The Student's Guide to the Internet

Ian Winship
Information Services Department,
University of Northumbria at Newcastle

Alison McNab
Pilkington Library, Loughborough University

Library Association Publishing
London

Published by
Library Association Publishing
7 Ridgmount Street
London WC1E 7AE

First published 1996

British Library Cataloguing in Publication Data
A catalogue record for this book is available from the British Library

ISBN 1-85604-207-3

Library Association Publishing offer their grateful thanks for the support of the Joint Information Systems Committee (JISC) of the Higher Education Funding Councils for this publication

Typeset from authors' disk in Elegant Garamond and Geometric 415 by Library Association Publishing
Printed and made in Great Britain by Bookcraft (Bath) Ltd, Midsomer Norton, Avon.

Contents

Introduction

Yes, another book on the Internet to add to the hundreds already published! So what makes this one different?

★ It is British.

Most books about the Internet originate in the USA, and although the Internet is international they still have a US bias in the information sources they cover. This one includes important UK sources you are unlikely to see in other books.

★ It is for students – and others in higher and further education.

We emphasize the Internet as an information resource, and feature those sources most useful to support academic courses – including those available only to UK higher education. Because the book is short and concise it is affordable too! We don't specifically consider recreational and leisure information, but what you learn will be useful for finding that too.

★ It is realistic.

We don't claim that all you ever need to know is on the Internet, but we do show you what is important and how Internet resources complement other printed and electronic sources of information.

Our aim is simply to get you started using the Internet. We cannot tell you all you will ever need to know, but we can – and do – show you the main procedures and sources to help you explore the Internet, build up your knowledge of how to use it, and find how it can be relevant to your particular needs.

We cannot deal with all the local variations of accessing the Internet, so we do not discuss how to connect to it; nor can we do more than outline, for example, the principles of the many electronic mail systems in use or the main features of Web browsers. You will need to find fuller practical details from your local computing service or library.

While it would also be nice to offer a comprehensive guide to subject information, to do so would need a book ten times the size, and much of the content would date rapidly, so we illustrate what is available and discuss major collections of subject information for you to consult. In general we try to demonstrate principles and give examples, with suggested sources to go to for further information. Your own institution may well have a World Wide Web server providing local information and access to the Internet. If so, this will give you an easy route to many of the sources we discuss.

Since the Internet changes all the time, and sources (or sites as they are often known) come and go, we have tried to concentrate on the more established, stable and general sources that should be around for some time, in particular those for UK education. Higher and further education receives its money from the government through organizations called funding councils who wish to encourage the use of networked information and so finance various services for the education community. These are discussed mostly in Chapter 5 and are the sources you might find most relevant to begin with.

We have checked the sources listed during the preparation of the book, but because of the ever-changing nature of the Internet we cannot guarantee that all the addresses (URLs) given will still be valid when you try to use them.

Ian Winship
Alison McNab

1

What is the Internet and how can it help you?

- ★ Access to the Internet
- ★ The Internet's vital statistics
- ★ What you will and won't find on the Internet

The Economist magazine announced in December 1992 that 'if you're not on the Net, you're not in the know'.[1] Since then many millions of words have been written about the Internet, which has caught the public imagination in a way few other technologies have, even though access is still available only to a minority.

So what is it? Well, contrary to what some have said, it is not – yet – the greatest information source ever with the answers to all your questions. Simply put, the Internet is an international network of computer networks – it links millions of computers around the world, and can be used for many different and ever-growing purposes. It can be seen as an extension to your campus network, in that it allows you to access different types of information (documents and software, for example) as if they were held on your own computer, and other people can read documents you choose to 'publish' on the Internet as if they were held on their own machine.

Students and staff in higher education are in a privileged position in having ready access to the Internet through **JANET** (the Joint Academic NETwork) which links higher education, part of further education, and research centres in the UK. You will have

[1]'The good network guide', *The Economist,* 26 December 1992 – 8 January 1993, 26.

access through your institution to one or more local area networks (the campus network), which provides links to JANET, and so to the Internet. **SuperJANET** is the upgraded version of JANET which offers greater speed and capacity.

This book discusses two main ways in which you can use the Internet: to **communicate** with other people, and to find **information**.

Communication can take the form of using electronic mail to correspond with family and friends in other cities, an 'expert' somewhere or your tutor while you are on industrial placement or on a year abroad (see Chapter 3). It can also consist of publishing your CV or part of your final-year project on the World Wide Web (see Chapter 11).

The sort of information which can be located on the Internet ranges from data to assist in writing that final-year project (see Chapter 5) to adverts for jobs after you graduate (see Chapter 7). Chapters 8 and 9 explain complementary ways of searching for information.

Background

The Internet as we know it today developed from an experimental computer networks in the USA in the early 1970s. Standard techniques enable different types of computer running different software to talk to one other and exchange data (information), so forming the seamless network which we know as the Internet. The information that you send to other people (perhaps as an electronic mail message), or that someone requests from a host computer, is despatched by the software along what is perceived to be the most appropriate route, from network to network until it reaches the required destination.

Client/server technology underlies much of the Internet. Server computers disseminate information resources, and these are retrieved by client machines on global or local computer networks. In other words, you run a client program on your workstation which opens connections to remote computers, requests data from them, and receives and displays the resulting information. The server software runs on the remote computer you access, and can normally handle information requests from many clients simultaneously.

As a student, you will normally find that support staff on campus will handle the technology and communications on your behalf. If you encounter problems, you should report them using the normal procedures for doing so on your campus – a fault cannot be fixed until it has been notified, but bear in mind that not all faults can be fixed instantly!

No one organization or individual controls the Internet, and for this reason it is often described as anarchic. Nevertheless, there are key individuals and groups who monitor the Internet and who have influenced its development. The Internet Society or ISOC is a non-governmental international organization for global cooperation and coordination for the Internet and its internetworking technologies and applications. Its Internet address or **URL** (explained in Chapter 4) is:

http://info.isoc.org/

It sponsors the Internet Engineering Task Force (IETF), which discusses operational and technical issues relating to the Internet, and the Internet Architecture Board (IAB), which allocates addresses and agrees on standards.

The Internet was originally used mainly by education and military research, but the recent huge growth in commercial use means that other organizations are having more influence. Computer companies like Microsoft and Netscape market Internet products such as browsers (see Chapter 4), that by their widespread use set standards that others have to meet to compete.

Access to the Internet

Students in higher education in the UK are fortunate to have Internet access which is 'free at the point of use', because it has been paid for by the Funding Councils. You will therefore only incur costs if you wish to dial in to your campus network from where you live, although an increasing number of halls of residence are being 'wired' to provide access for students with their own computer workstations.

Your institution will place some restrictions on your Internet usage. While some of these will be related to resourcing (e.g. you are likely to be allocated a finite amount of file storage space), others will relate to acceptable use and copyright. Chapter 3 discusses some aspects of **netiquette** or network etiquette, while Chapter 11 touches on the JANET Acceptable Use Policy. Your fellow students and your institution may suffer if you breach either the local or national guidelines on use of the Internet. Staff in your library or computing service should be able to advise you on local access conditions on campus, as well as providing guidelines on using the Internet effectively.

If you have your own computer workstation (with a modem or network card, and the appropriate software), you may be able to plug it into your campus network, which will have a link to JANET and thus to the Internet. Even if you don't have your own workstation, your institution will provide access to workstations, some of which may be available 24 hours a day.

During your vacations you may feel you want to have occasional access to the Internet – this is possible in many towns through the growing number of **cyber cafés**, which provide fixed-rate access to a terminal with an Internet connection. An up-to-date listing of United Kingdom cyber cafés is available from *Internet* magazine – you can receive information by sending an e-mail message to:

internet.cafes@computing.emap.co.uk

or the latest latest list can be found using their *What's New in the UK* search tool, selecting the *Cyber Cafés, Pubs, etc.* option:

http://www.emap.com/whatsnew/search.htm

If you are a part-time student you may want Internet access from home or work, and once you leave higher education you may likewise want continued Internet access. You will need to learn new techniques for minimizing the amount of time you spend online, and you will have to find a commercial Internet Service Provider (ISP) instead of using JANET. There is a plethora of different companies who vie to offer Internet access, with many tempting introductory offers. If you envisage spending a fair amount of time online, it may be more economical to choose one of the companies that offers a fixed monthly charge, irrespective of how much time you spend online. Typical costs might be a £10–£20 setup charge, then a similar amount per month in addition to local phone calls.

For the latest information on Internet Service Providers, you should consult the monthly magazines about the Internet that are published in the UK (see Chapter 13). One useful listing of Internet Service Providers in the UK can be found at:

    http://thelist.iworld.com/country/United_Kingdom.html

Be careful not to commit yourself to one Internet Service Provider for too long a period initially, as you may wish to change ISP as your knowledge increases and your requirements change.

Some statistics

We all know that statistics can be made to prove anything and those for the Internet are less precise than most, having mainly to rely on estimates. Nonetheless, here are just a few to give a flavour for the size and growth of the Internet.

    Netree Internet Statistics
    http://www.netree.com/netbin/internetstats
estimate that by mid-1996 over 70 million people had access to the Internet.

    MIDS (Matrix Information and Directory Services)
    http://www.mids.org/mids/
publish Internet demographic surveys and have estimated that the number of people on the Internet has doubled every year since the early 1990s.

The typical Internet user is often stereotyped as being male, a graduate, and in the 20–30 age range. Demographic trends bear this out to some extent, but these are always changing as access to the Internet increases. The estimate of the proportion of female users on the Internet varies from 29% to 36% according to *Cyberatlas*

http://www.cyberatlas.com/demographics.html

Concern that a growing number of Internet users are developing Internet addiction is borne out by studies revealing that some people spend more than 40 hours a week online (*Cyberatlas*).

'More Internet access is from work (or university or college) than from home, but this is estimated to become evened out by the year 2000' – International Data Corp

http://www.idcresearch.com/idc.htm

From a survey they had conducted in the USA and Canada, Nielsen Media Research

http://www.nielsenmedia.com/

estimated that over 2.7 million people had used the Internet for shopping. Commercial use of the Internet has been primarily in the following areas: computer products, travel, entertainment, clothing, gifts, and food and drink.

Commercial use of the Internet is reflected in services such as the *UK Directory*, which lists over 6,000 such sites in the UK:

http://www.ukdirectory.com/

The relevant section of Yahoo (see Chapter 8) includes links to a variety of services which provide these statistics:

http://www.yahoo.com/Computers_and_Internet/
Internet/Statistics_and_Demographics/

What you will and won't find on the Internet

In general, information that costs a lot to collect and create, such as marketing and other financial data, or that is primarily of commercial value is unlikely to be available free of charge on the Internet, except where there are special arrangements for higher education (see Chapter 5). What you may find are trial or cut-down versions of software, earlier versions of documents, or sections of reports. While selling services and goods over the Internet has not proved to be the money-spinner some companies had hoped it would be, many organizations feel that they at least require an **Internet presence** and an increasing number of advertisements in all forms of the media include URLs. These company sites can be disappointing, and may give little more information than a 30-second TV commercial. Others, particularly those from high-tech companies, will provide valuable, useful data.

Ultimately, any information that you find on the Internet is only as good as the provider makes it. It is important to be critical in relation to resources that you find on the Internet, whether these are Web pages, databases or software. You need to consider whether these are accurate, comprehensive and up-to-date – the best Web pages, for example, will include information about the individual or organization which authored them as well as the date on which they were last updated. There is a difference between facts and opinions – learning to distinguish between these is important, but perhaps never more so than on the Internet. Many companies will be seeking future employees who have gained familiarity with the Internet and electronic communication while students, and the ability to think critically is one of the most valuable benefits a graduate can bring to an organization.

Where the Internet has proved to be invaluable is in relation to information that will not be static for long enough to be published in printed form (such as the list of cyber cafés mentioned on page 4) or that needs to be updated regularly (such as sports results). Much information that is ephemeral and with little long-term value is ideal for distributing via the Internet. Individuals with the time and interest to collect information on their hobbies or leisure interests have found the Internet an ideal medium through which to provide newsletters, fanzines, facts and figures, and even software. However, enthusiasm and circumstances can change, so these types of source can be short-lived.

Topics that have a high profile in the media and the professional press tend to be prominent on the Internet as well. Thus you will find many Web pages which deal with all aspects of AIDS, the environment, computers and the Internet itself.

The Internet is sometimes used for distributing resources found in another medium – as a growing range of Internet versions of daily newspapers and magazines demonstrates (see Chapter 6).

To trace books and journal articles for essays and assignments, you will almost certainly have more success if you use your library catalogue or **OPAC** (online public access catalogue), and seek the advice of library staff on the best indexing/abstracting services to use (see Chapter 5). Alternatively, you may well use the Internet to access your OPAC (or one at a nearby library) or one of the *BIDS* or *FirstSearch* databases. However, you will normally still have to go and fetch the book you want from the library shelves. More and more academic journals are becoming available in electronic formats, and your institution is likely to be participating in a national initiative to promote access to **electronic journals**.

There is also a growing range of services which will offer to post, fax or e-mail the full text of journal articles (such as *UnCover*, discussed in Chapter 5) but these should only be used in emergencies as you will have to bear the cost yourself. Always check whether your library subscribes to the journal in question, and, if it does not, enquire about the **interlibrary loan facilities** available to you.

As early access to the Internet was most widespread amongst the academic and research community, it is not surprising that much information to be found on the Internet reflects this. Most universities and colleges now provide extensive information about their courses and research activities. In higher education, most articles and books have gone through a process of evaluation by other experts in the field (this is known as peer review). How to replicate this process for Internet resources originating in the research community is still being considered. There are some researchers who feel that the results of publicly-funded academic work should remain in the public domain free of charge, and several **pre-print archives** (see Chapter 6) illustrate this. There is a tension between those who see the Internet as a commercial opportunity and those who see it as a distribution medium for information, open to everyone in the same way a public library is, but on a global scale.

This book discusses different information resources found on the Internet that will be of use to you in your studies and beyond. The types of resources available include:

★ **text**: reports, articles, books, directories and databases
★ **images**: graphics, photographs and video clips
★ **sound**
★ **software**: freeware, shareware, evaluation copies and upgrades of commercial products
★ **junk**!

Although there is much talk of the 'electronic campus' or 'digital library', most academic institutions are still only beginning to explore the real possibilities and opportunities opened up by widespread access to the Internet. You will still read and generate much paper during your time as a student, but you can use networked resources to enhance the traditional sources of information to which you have access, to trace a lot of 'non-traditional' information, and to 'network' with people. The Internet makes the 'global village' more of a possibility than ever before, and during your time as a student you have the opportunity to explore and contribute to this – don't miss out!

2

Understanding and using Internet addresses

★ How Internet addresses are constructed
★ Why you need to know

Each computer on the Internet has a unique **address** (similar to a postal address or a phone number) to allow users to contact it. The Internet Protocol, or IP, address is made up of 4 sets of digits, e.g. 192.112.36.5. However, it is difficult for people to remember these numbers, so a variant system using names has become universal – you will rarely see an address in the numerical format.

These addresses are created in a database called the Domain Name System (DNS) and follow prescribed patterns.

All addresses have at least two parts – an organization name, and the domain, the type of organization, but may have three, four or five parts.

A typical address is that for the library catalogue at the University of Northumbria:

opac.unn.ac.uk

The parts of the address represent a particular **computer** – **opac** – at a particular **organization** – the University of Northumbria, here abbreviated to **unn** – in the **academic** domain – **ac** – and in a particular **country** – the UK, by convention printed in lower-case letters – **uk**.

Other examples of academic addresses in the UK are:

ukoln.bath.ac.uk

a computer named UKOLN at the University of Bath

cs.staffs.ac.uk
the Computer Science department at Staffordshire University.

Non-academic organizations have other codes for their domain, e.g.

pavilion.co.uk
a company

bbcnc.org.uk
a non-profit organization: the BBC

coi.gov.uk
a government body: the Central Office of Information

Foreign addresses have a different country code:

info.funet.fi
Finland

www.springer.de
Germany

The exception is the USA, where you will rarely see the **us** code used. This is because they invented the Internet, just as British postage stamps have no country name because we invented them! Some international organizations are starting to use an **int** code.

US addresses differ also in their 3-character domain names:

www.whitehouse.gov
government

dialog.com
a company

comics.scs.unr.edu
an educational establishment

rs.internic.net
a network administrative body

nic.ddn.mil
a military organization

pubs.acs.org
a non-profit organization

Confusingly, some UK-based organizations now also use the **.com** and **.org** domains, for example the *Economist* magazine at

http://www.economist.com

We are also beginning to see variations such as **uk.com**, and the commercialization of the Internet may well allow domains like **.ibm** or **.clothes**

Using addresses

You will need to use addresses when sending electronic mail (see Chapter 3) and when connecting to various remote resources using telnet or on the World Wide Web (see Chapter 4). However, for much of the time you may not need to key them in as your local Web service will include the most popular ones, and you will build up your own collection of those you find most useful in a 'bookmark' list or 'hotlist'.

Nevertheless, it is always useful to know how addresses are put together. Sometimes you may spot a mistake in an address or you may not know the address of some particular organization you want to contact but can make a good guess what it might be. So a WWW (World Wide Web) machine usually has an address in the form www.name.domain.country, e.g.:

www.ox.ac.uk

and commercial companies like to include an obvious version of their name, e.g.:

www.j-sainsbury.co.uk

Finding addresses

There is no overall list of Internet addresses to consult, but there are various ways of finding them.

If you need an address for electronic mail then some sources are discussed in Chapter 3. If you want to connect to a particular organization, and guessing the likely form of the address does not work, then you can try the World Wide Web search services discussed in Chapter 9. These index millions of pages of information on the Internet, so will generally find those from any organization you specify and show the address. In some cases the search can be limited to words in the address only, and not in the text of pages, so simplifying the process.

3

Essential communication skills on the Net

★ Using electronic mail to communicate with individuals
★ Using discussion lists and newsgroups to share information and experience on a subject
★ Network etiquette – good practice in using mail

Electronic mail

The most accessible use of the Internet is to communicate with other users worldwide using electronic mail.

Electronic mail, or **e-mail**, is a means of sending a message – from a few lines to many pages – from your computer, or more likely from the space allocated to you on your departmental or institutional system, to someone else's space elsewhere. This person's space may be in your own institution or anywhere on the Internet. The process is generally quick – a few seconds to reach someone in your own institution; minutes, hours, or perhaps longer, to the other side of the world.

You simply type in your message and the address to which it is to be sent, and send the message. The recipient has to check his/her 'mailbox' to see what messages have been received – it's a bit like a telephone answering machine. The most popular – if not strictly academic – use will be to keep in touch with your friends in other institutions free of charge, but you may also be able to contact your lecturers in this way, or experts in other places.

To use e-mail you need to contact your computing service to get an account (no money is involved!) on your local computer system which will have a mail facility. There are many different ones, such as Pine, Eudora, Pegasus, Microsoft Mail and VMS. Some use a Windows environment with menus to choose options from, others will require you to enter commands. Detailed procedures cannot be given here but your computing service will provide instructions.

All mail systems should allow you to:

★ edit a message offline before you send it
★ reply to one received, quoting text from the original message if desired
★ forward one to someone else
★ store messages for future reference, if necessary in folders or directories
★ print messages
★ delete messages
★ create a mailing list to send a message to a group of people
★ send a file of text already created
★ save a message you have received as a file so that you can edit it
★ set up an 'alias' – a short form of address – for frequently used addresses

Figure 3.1 shows a typical message with a lot of information at the beginning (the header) relating to the route the message has taken. This may not always be present, or may be hidden by the software. Your address is normally added automatically but you should include your name (and, if appropriate, your organization) and address at the end. Some people use a signature file like this one giving more information, or even a witty quote, which can be added automatically or easily to your message.

You should always put a useful title in the **Subject:** line. Many people get lots of messages a day and will scan their list of messages to see which to read first – or maybe delete uninteresting-looking ones without reading them.

You need to manage your messages since you may have limited

```
From lbe408@coventry.ac.uk Tue Feb 20 13:41:53 1996
Received: from leofric.coventry.ac.uk by norn.ncl.ac.uk id <NAA16903@norn.ncl.ac.uk>
  (with ESMTP; Tue, 20 Feb 1996 13:41:46 GMT
  Received: (from lbe408@localhost) by leofric.coventry.ac.uk (8.6.12/8.6.11) id NAA06998; Tue, 20 Feb 1996
13:41:14 GMT
Date: Tue, 20 Feb 1996 13:41:14 +0000 (GMT)
From: "J.Smith" <lbe408@coventry.ac.uk>
X-Sender: lbe408@leofric
To: alan.shearer@ncl.ac.uk
Subject: videos and multimedia
Message-ID: <Pine.OSF.3.91.960220133955.10883A-100000@leofric>
MIME-Version: 1.0
Content-Type: TEXT/PLAIN; charset=US-ASCII
Reply-To: "J.Smith" <lbe408@coventry.ac.uk>
Precedence: list


Alan

I've had a request for information about teaching/learning videos,
software or multimedia packages suitable for higher education in the fields of
physics or materials science. Most directories I've looked at seem to be aimed
at schools, and the Internet sources I've tried via NISS (CTI, TLTP etc),
although potentially useful, still seem to be at an early stage.
Any suggestions?

John
-----------------------------------------------------------------
I    John Smith                                               I
I    Physical Sciences  Librarian                            I
I    Lanchester Library        tel: 01203 81690              I
I    Coventry University       fax: 01203 81686              I
I    Much Park Street          e-mail: lbe408@coventry.ac.uk I
I    Coventry   CV1 2HF                                       I
-----------------------------------------------------------------
```

Fig. 3.1 *An e-mail message*

space for storing them. You should get into the habit of checking
your message files and deleting those you no longer need.

E-mail addresses

In Chapter 2 we showed how the address for a particular computer
is formed. An e-mail address simply adds the identity of the person
concerned in the form **person@place**. This identity may be a string
of characters like **vhf45**, which will usually be your ID to log on to
your local system, or it may be a more meaningful real name.

Examples:
vhf45@gold.ac.uk
j.smith@leeds.ac.uk
mary.green@cs.wsu.edu

Finding addresses

E-mail addresses are allocated by the institution concerned so there are no comprehensive national directories as there are for telephone numbers. Finding someone's address may be tricky, but there are a number of places to try, although they may not always be helpful for students' addresses. You can search on first and last names, and maybe a place or organization too.

JANET Directory Service
telnet://directory.ja.net
login: **dua**

This covers many UK universities, but is cumbersome to use and inconsistent in what it finds – sometimes it won't find addresses that it has found previously.

Four11 E-Mail Directory
http://www.four11.com

You can use this directory to search for other people's addresses from countries throughout the world, and to add your own. You will need to register the first time you use the system. A guide to searching is available.

There are lots of other directories based on various published sources of addresses. They vary in their accuracy and may include out-of-date addresses. Try:

Internet Address Finder
http://www.iaf.net

Okra
http://okra.ucr.edu/okra

Bigfoot
http://www.bigfoot.com

Search Usenet addresses
http://usenet-addresses.mit.edu

Web Form
http://http1.brunel.ac.uk:8080/x500/search-form-gb.htm

Web Form allows you to search for addresses of individuals and organizations in the UK. A similar form allows searches for people and organizations worldwide.

Mailbase

http://www.mailbase.ac.uk

The *Mailbase* service (discussed below) can be used to find the addresses of people who have subscribed to their discussion lists. These will mostly be in the UK.

If you know the institution someone belongs to – particularly a university – you may be able to find details on its WWW service. (See Chapter 4 for lists of WWW services.)

Discussion lists

A discussion list uses e-mail to create a world-wide forum to

★ discuss topics
★ ask and answer questions
★ pass on news
★ share information on a particular subject

and so on.

A similar function is provided by Usenet newsgroups (see page 21), with each list or newsgroup dealing with a particular topic area.

Lists tend to cover academic subjects more than newsgroups do, though there are also many for recreational topics. Subjects are as varied as:

★ dance
★ databases
★ dentistry

★ Derrida

★ disarmament

A list will be based in one country – most are in the USA – but open for anyone anywhere to join, though the membership and content, may reflect that country. Some are intended particularly for students, such as

humgrad@Mailbase.ac.uk

and

arch-student@lists.colorado.edu for archaeologists.

You choose if you wish to join a list, and do so by sending an e-mail message to an address to register.

The message will be something like

subscribe econ-model Bill Brown

(if your name is Bill Brown).

(You do not need to include your e-mail address as that is extracted automatically.)

You send this message to an address in the form:

listserv@thvm.cmu.edu

majordomo@thvm.cmu.edu

for most US-based lists

or **mailbase@mailbase.ac.uk**

for those on *Mailbase*

Registration is done automatically by a program and you will receive confirmation and instructions on how to use the list. However, there is always a person – the list owner – whom you can contact if you have problems.

Messages are sent to the list address and normally are distributed to all those who are registered on the list. (Some lists are 'moderated' and messages are processed by a person – usually to give some co-ordination, but occasionally to control what is being sent.) There is no obligation to contribute to a list, and you will probably benefit just from 'listening in' to the discussion or reading news items. Some hints on good practice in using lists can be found later in this chapter.

Finding what lists there are

There are thousands of lists out there, and a number of directories exist to help you discover them. They will always include instructions on how to join a particular list. Be aware that lists do not exist for every subject you might want.

Academically oriented lists in Britain are mostly part of the *Mailbase* project based at Newcastle University. They have a central service

http://www.mailbase.ac.uk

that lists all their lists and for each gives a description, a directory of all the members, and an archive of messages that have been sent to the list. You can search list names and descriptions by subject. If you find a list that looks relevant, you can check the message archive to see what sort of topics are discussed before deciding whether to join. (Figure 3.2 shows a section from a list of messages on the Tourism list.)

Other directories have a worldwide coverage but do not include lists of members or message archives.

The *Directory of Scholarly Electronic Conferences* at

http://www.n2h2.com/KOVACS

is produced regularly by a team led by Diane Kovacs at Kent State University and concentrates on scholarly lists worldwide. Only a brief description is included. You can search list names and descriptions or browse the lists for a subject area.

research into US travel distribution	CHRIS HOLLOWAY
CHILDREN EXCHANGE	Sylvie IRIS
Competition for natural resources	Paul Jeffrey
(fwd) Report: Casinos drain local economy	Robert J Conlan
visitor expenditure models	bryan.hughes
visitor expenditure models -Reply	(fwd) bryan.hughes
Heritage Visitor Attractions : An Operations	
Management.	Anna Leask
PACIFIC TOURISM REVIEW - Invitation for	
special reports	MARTIN OPPERMANN

Fig. 3.2 *Directory of messages in the archive of the Mailbase Tourism list*

For a directory of all types of list try *Liszt*
http://www.liszt.com/
which has over 50,000 lists indexed or *Tile.Net*
http://tile.net/lists
which includes the Usenet groups described below.

Usenet newsgroups

Usenet is one of the oldest uses of the Internet, being created in 1979 by students in North America who wished to link together people using the Unix operating system, who shared common interests. Today it is a conferencing system in which any user can participate in the discussion of a wide range of topics covered by **newsgroups**. Each newsgroup contains **articles** or messages which may be grouped in **threads** or themes. It has a similar function to discussion lists, and users can post (send) and reply to messages, mail interesting articles to themselves and usually access newsgroup archives. As with lists, some newsgroups are **moderated**, which means that articles are screened for approval before appearing in the newsgroup.

Usenet is in essence a huge continuously updated database that users must consult to read messages – they do not arrive in a mailbox. It requires a very large amount of storage space, so your university is likely to offer only a selection of newsgroups for access, probably limiting this to those which are primarily of academic interest. You can look at any of the newsgroups but will normally **subscribe** to (select) those you want to see regularly – only these will be displayed when you connect.

There are over 15,000 newsgroups available, and the number grows daily, covering leisure interests as much as academic subjects. Newsgroup names are organized in hierarchies with a number of categories, including:

alt   'alternative' discussions
biz   business
bionet   biological sciences

comp	computer hardware and software, computer science
news	news about Usenet
rec	hobbies and leisure interests
sci	research in the sciences
soc	social issues and world cultures
uk	newsgroups specifically on UK topics

Some examples are **alt.lefthanders, misc.health.therapy.occupational,** and **uk.media.tv.sf.drwho**

To access newsgroups you will require software known as a *newsreader*. In some cases this may be a text-based reader (such as *tin* or *pine*). However, recent versions of the Netscape WWW browser include a function for reading newsgroups, and this is a very effective way to browse them. Or you can download FreeAgent (for home or evaluation use) from

http://www.forteinc.com/forte

– this is a useful offline newsreader.

Your computing service is likely to provide documentation on using Usenet and the newsreader(s) available locally.

Figure 3.3 shows a typical list of messages using the *tin* newsreader.

```
sci.bio.fisheries (9T 10A 0K 0H R)            h=help

  1 + 2  House Votes For Dolphin Death Act       Ken Yarborough- Ea
  2 +    Info wanted on Juvenile fish             Genders A J
  3 +    Preservation of Biological Samples       murray darrach
  4 +    smallmouth bass habitat                  Erik
  5 +    Cyanide Bibliography - Fishes and Corals Don McAllister
  6 +    Nitrate Removal From Sea Water           James A. Mackie
  7 +    Salmon Recovery - The Lack of Recovery   Mark Booker
  8 +    Wholesale bait manufacturers             Roland Close
  9 +    Eco-fisheries papers                     Don McAllister

  <n>=set current to n, TAB=next unread, /=search pattern, ^K)ill/select,
a)uthor search, c)atchup, j)line down, k=line up, K=mark read, l)ist thread,
 |=pipe, m)ail, o=print, q)uit, r=toggle all/unread, s)ave, t)ag, w=post
```

Fig. 3.3 *List of messages on the sci.bio.fisheries newsgroup using the* tin *newsreader*

It is possible to spend (or waste!) a lot of time reading and contributing to newsgroups – while you may wish to keep up with newsgroups that are particularly relevant to your academic or spare time interests, do remember that there is life beyond Usenet!

Identifying newsgroups of potential interest can be done in a variety of ways – you can simply browse down the hierarchies accessible to you, or consult a listing such as *Directory of scholarly electronic conferences* or *Tile.Net* (see pages 19–20).

Not all institutions provide access to newsgroups, but you can access public Usenet services at, for example, Birmingham University

gopher://gopher.bham.ac.uk/11/Usenet

to read, print, copy to disk or e-mail messages to yourself – you cannot send messages to a newsgroup. Newsreader software is not needed.

Each site that offers Usenet newsgroups will make its own decision about which newsgroups to offer and the size of newsgroup archives which it will make available. Because of the storage requirements some may keep only a week or two's messages, so you need to get into a regular routine of checking the newsgroups that interest you. It is possible to search the archives of the majority of newsgroups using services such as *DejaNews* or *Alta Vista* (see Chapter 9). These searching tools make it possible to search for messages posted by particular individuals as well as for those on specific topics. You should therefore be cautious of the content of messages you post to newsgroups; as messages you post may be viewed by supervisors or potential employers. If in doubt it is probably best not to post.

Background information for new users of Usenet can be found in the

news.announce.newusers

newsgroup. This newsgroup normally includes regular postings of articles entitled 'What is Usenet?' and 'Frequently asked questions about Usenet'. The latter is an example of a **FAQ** or **Frequently asked questions**. FAQs are introductory files of information on a topic reflecting the commonest questions people ask about it. Since newsgroups range in subject from the erudite to the exotic, FAQs can deal with topics such as Ben Elton, how to become an astronaut, and US government information on the Web. Each FAQ is distributed on one or more relevant newsgroups and should be updated and reissued regularly. There are collections of them such as that at Oxford University

    http://www.lib.ox.ac.uk/Internet/news/faq/by_group.index.
    html

You can browse by category or newsgroup or search the whole collection.

Netiquette

Netiquette, or network etiquette, refers to the generally accepted standards of good practice in using e-mail, discussion lists and newsgroups. There is a need for some discipline to ensure that lists work effectively and that time and computer useage is not wasted. The following are some useful guidelines:

★ Remember that mail systems are not especially secure or necessarily private, so don't use e-mail for confidential or otherwise sensitive communication. Think of a mail message as being similar to a message written on a postcard. Remember also that messages can usually be traced back to the sender.

★ Lists and newsgroups are intended to be a civilized forum, and the bad temper, abuse or anger that might occur in a face-to-face discussion is not appreciated. (Such electronic anger is usually known as 'flaming'.) Remember that the law can be applied to electronic communication, so don't make comments about someone that could, for example, be libellous or racist.

★ Do not ask trivial questions on a list that could be answered more easily in other ways (e.g. by looking in a book). They are likely to be ignored.

★ Do not ask questions that would require someone to do your research or write your assignment for you. Ask specific questions, if necessary telling people what you already know, and don't expect long or comprehensive answers. A response is more likely from someone if it can draw on their experience.

★ Nevertheless, do not be inhibited by feeling ignorant or overawed by the presence of academic staff on lists – many others are beginners too. 'I'm new to this list so this may have been asked before' is often a useful introduction.

★ Be considerate to others and allow for their mistakes. Do not reprimand people for not understanding procedures properly.

★ Brief comments are more likely to be widely read and to generate replies.

★ Try to respond to queries if you have something to contribute – lack of response is disheartening.

★ Lists can be a useful place to distribute questionnaires, but keep them short and don't expect a huge response. Remember that a list membership will not be a properly constituted sample.

★ Do not send 'chain letters': they are an abuse of the system that can slow down mail for others.

If you want more extensive guidelines try *The Net: user guidelines and netiquette* by Arlene Rinaldi
http://www.fau.edu/rinaldi/net/index.htm

4

Net techniques explained

★ Telnet, gopher, World Wide Web, file transfer
  protocol, Archie
★ How they work and what to use them for

Telnet

Telnet is the basic Internet command used to make a simple connection to a computer somewhere. Typically this computer will have some sort of large searchable database, such as a library catalogue, a collection of references on a subject or statistical information.

If you are using a command line interface, the telnet command is made from the system prompt, such as a $ or %, in the form

  telnet *address*

For example, you type

  telnet bids.ac.uk

for the *BIDS* databases, or

  telnet fedworld.gov

for US government bulletin boards.

Alternatively you key **telnet** to get a **telnet>** prompt and then enter the address.

If you use a graphical environment you will have an icon for telnet which you double-click on and then enter the address in a dialog box.

Occasionally you will also have to enter a username or password, but you will normally be shown on the screen what this is. (It will be the same for everyone.)

You may also be asked for a terminal type, perhaps choosing from a list. Unless you know otherwise reply **VT100**. (The terminal type affects the screen layout, so if the layout is not right – for example, if it contains garbled characters – then you have the wrong terminal type.)

Telnet software includes a large range of commands, most of which you are unlikely to need, other than:

CONTROL-B to send a break or interrupt command to the remote system if you need to stop some process, perhaps because you have made a mistake

CONTROL-Q to quit from telnet **quit** to return to the system prompt from the **telnet>** prompt

You can see a list of the commands by keying help at the **telnet>** prompt.

You will find that the databases you connect to with telnet may all be different in the way they work, so you will probably need some instructions on how to use them. These may be available online or in printed form from your library or computing service.

There is no complete directory of addresses of 'telnetable' resources, but a useful route to many, including bulletin boards, library catalogues and databases, is *Hytelnet*. Telnet to **rsl.ox.ac.uk** and login as **hytelnet**, or use the World Wide Web version at **http://www.cam.ac.uk/Hytelnet**.

This gives you lists from which you can connect to the service you want. To find other services using telnet, check the subject guides discussed in Chapter 8.

Gopher

Gopher software was developed to simplify access and organization of information on the Internet, but it has now been largely replaced by the World Wide Web. The name may derive from the name of the football team at the University of Minnesota, where the software was devised, or from the fact that it 'goes fer' things on the Internet.

Gopher is not only a connection command like telnet but is also a standardized way of presenting the information using a hierarchy of menus. Users move down the hierarchy to more specific subjects.

With a WWW graphical browser (see the next section), you merely click on the menu title to follow a particular menu and on the slider bar to move up and down a page. Use the **Back** button to go back up the hierarchy.

With text-based systems you can key the menu number or use the arrow keys to move up and down the list and then press Return. Move back up a level with **U** or the left arrow. The space bar takes you to the next page and **B** to the previous one.

A full list of commands can be found online. They include the ability to mail a file to yourself or to download one to your PC or filespace.

Menus on a gopher system may refer to information held at that organization or may link to information on other parts of the Internet without the user needing to key in an address . Selecting an item causes the system to make (usually successfully!) a gopher or telnet connection to that information source. If the system is having difficulty connecting to a source, then delete the request with the Stop button in a graphical browser or (when using text-based gopher software) by keying **CONTROL-C** and replying **N** to the query on quitting.

To connect from a command prompt, key

gopher *address*

For example, you might type

gopher gopher.phil.ruu.nl

With a Web browser, enter a URL (see the next section) in the form

gopher://gopher.phil.ruu.nl

Depending on how you connect, the initial screen will look something like Figure 4.1

```
Internet Gopher Information Client v2.0.12

              Root gopher server: gopher.phil.ruu.nl

  -->  1. Department of Philosophy - Utrecht University
       2. Bibliographies/
       3. Computer Info/
       4. Electronic journals (info & links)/
       5. Electronic texts/
       6. Dutch Research School for Advanced Studies in Ethics/
       7. Frequently asked questions (FAQ - new.answers)/
       8. Journals/
       9. Mailing list archives/
      10. Mailing list descriptions/
      11. Miscellaneous/
      12. Network Info/
      13. Phone books and E-mail addresses/
      14. WETFIL/


      15. Your gateway to the world .../




Press ? for Help, q to Quit
Page: 1/1
```

Fig. 4.1 *Main screen of a gopher server*

Gopher systems have been very popular with universities and professional institutes and societies to display local information and to point to useful resources elsewhere.

There are lists of gopher services in the UK:

key **gopher ukoln.bath.ac.uk**

and choose

UK gopher servers

from the main menu

and for the whole world :

key **gopher gopher.tc.umn.edu**

and choose

Other gophers and information servers

However, be aware that many of these services may no longer exist, are not updated or will have changed to using the World Wide Web.

You will rarely need to connect directly to a gopher service, but you will often find one incorporated in a WWW site when you come to a page headed 'Gopher menu'.

World Wide Web

The **World Wide Web** (often abbreviated to WWW or simply the Web) is a hypertext-based system for finding and accessing Internet resources; it is now the dominant way of using the Internet. It can provide access to a variety of Internet resources from the same interface, including FTP, gopher and Usenet newsgroups in addition to WWW sites.

The World Wide Web is a **distributed** (in that it is not based in any single location), **multimedia** (combining text, still and moving images, and sound), and **hypertext** (containing links to other documents, allowing information to be retrieved in a nonsequential way) **system**. It is thus a unique medium for communication and for publishing.

Documents for the WWW are written in **HTML (HyperText Markup Language)** – see Chapter 11 for further information.

Uniform Resource Locators (URLs)

The **URL** (or Uniform Resource Locator) is the Internet equivalent of a full postal address, and is used to connect to servers, sites or pages around the world. URLs are a standard method of naming or specifying any kind of information on the Internet. The client computer that you use only needs to know what **protocol** to expect of the desired information, and it retrieves it by that protocol. The user or Web author specifies the format and protocol (a set of data-exchange rules that computer systems use to talk to each other over the network) by using an appropriate URL.

Note that URLs are case sensitive, so take care when copying them down. Web pages with a ~ (the tilde sign) in the URL are normally personal pages provided by an individual.

A URL will usually specify three things:

<method>://<address>/<pathname>

<method> is the general kind of protocol or method used to retrieve the document. This will be **http** for HTML documents on

the WWW; **gopher** for gopher documents and directories; **ftp** for FTP servers; **news** for Usenet newsgroups; and **telnet** for telnet sessions. The method **file** can be used to refer to local files.

<address> refers to the computer (server) where the information or documents are stored. HTML, gopher and FTP documents all have a server on a specific host computer. Telnet sessions have a specific destination computer. Newsgroups are the only exception – instead of a hostname, you provide a newsgroup (for example, **news:news.answers**);

<pathname> refers to the directory or file where the information is to be found. A URL for a directory usually ends with a / and that for a file with .htm or .html

Here are some sample URLs and explanations:

http://www.timeshigher.newsint.co.uk/thisweek.html
An HTML document from the *Times Higher Education Supplement*, listing the contents of the current issue of the weekly newspaper.

ftp://rtfm.mit.edu/pub/usenet-by-group/news.answers/ftp-list/faq
An FTP file (actually an FAQ) at a computer at the Massachusetts Institute of Technology, in the sub-directory /pub/usenet-by-group/ news.answers/ftp-list/.

gopher://resu1.ulb.ac.be:70/00/.socgoph.ans
The gopher file .socgoph.ans (describing the EU-funded Socrates programme) at the gopher server at the Université Libre de Bruxelles in Belgium in the directory /00/.

telnet://wisdom.wellcome.ac.uk
The telnet address of the remote computer at the Wellcome Institute to log into the Wisdom service.

Browsers

To access the World Wide Web, you need **browser** software. By mid-1996, most UK higher education institutions were using **Netscape Navigator** as the standard browser on campus – partly because it is available for PC, Macintosh and Unix machines. However, if you have access to a PC with Windows95, you may be running Microsoft's **Internet Explorer.**

The browser which popularized the World Wide Web was **Mosaic**, which was widely used until the widespread adoption of Netscape in 1995.

These are all graphical browsers which will show images and colour.

Your institution may also provide access to a text-only version of the World Wide Web using the **Lynx** browser. Lynx is often used on a networked terminal rather than a PC, or to give access to the WWW when a terminal is not powerful enough to provide a graphical interface. If the information on the site you wish to consult is text-based, it may be far quicker to browse using Lynx, even though one of the main features of the Web is its multimedia dimension. Even in a graphical browser, many experienced net users choose to switch the *images* (pictures or graphics) off, since they are often merely decorative and slow down transfer. In this way you can operate a browser like Netscape in a similar way to Lynx. Unfortunately not all WWW sites are set up to allow viewing in text-only mode.

Browser features include the ability to:

★ copy (save) a file to disk – in text or html form.
★ print a file. If it contains images the process will be slow, and you may need a colour printer for best results.
★ search the text of the file currently displayed.
★ to cut and paste text to other applications, if you are in a graphical environment like Windows.
★ open/go to a specific URL that you key in.

★ interrrupt a slow or unsuccessful file transfer.

★ mail files to yourself. Some institutions may not allow mail from Netscape for security reasons.

Figure 4.2 shows the toolbar (row of icons) on Netscape; as you can see there are also drop-down menus.

Figure 4.3 shows a Web page using Lynx. Key **H** (help), then choose **Keystroke commands** for a list of Lynx commands.

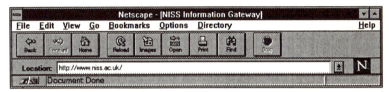

Fig. 4.2 *The toolbar on Netscape Navigator*

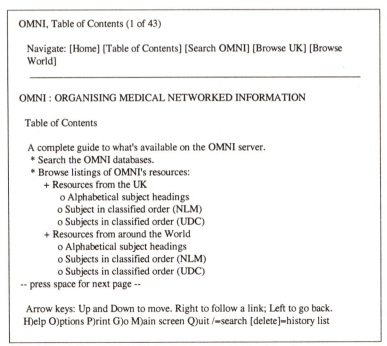

OMNI, Table of Contents (1 of 43)

Navigate: [Home] [Table of Contents] [Search OMNI] [Browse UK] [Browse World]

OMNI : ORGANISING MEDICAL NETWORKED INFORMATION

Table of Contents

A complete guide to what's available on the OMNI server.
  * Search the OMNI databases.
  * Browse listings of OMNI's resources:
    + Resources from the UK
        o Alphabetical subject headings
        o Subject in classified order (NLM)
        o Subjects in classified order (UDC)
    + Resources from around the World
        o Alphabetical subject headings
        o Subjects in classified order (NLM)
        o Subjects in classified order (UDC)
-- press space for next page --

Arrow keys: Up and Down to move. Right to follow a link; Left to go back.
H)elp O)ptions P)rint G)o M)ain screen Q)uit /=search [delete]=history list

Fig. 4.3 *A World Wide Web page seen with the Lynx browser*

The requirement of easy access to a wide variety of file formats (for example, Acrobat software for electronic journals), Internet services (e.g. Usenet news) and new programming languages such as Java, puts pressure on browser software to keep up. One solution is the development of modular browsers which allow additional **plug-in** or **helper** software to be added, so that you can, for example, view video clips or manipulate images of chemical molecules. On campus, you are unlikely to have the opportunity to customize, upgrade or even choose the browser software that you have access to, but it can be helpful to be aware that solutions may exist, even if they cannot be readily implemented on your campus network.

If you are particularly interested in browsers then *BrowserWatch* is a WWW site which collects information about browsers and plug-ins. In addition to providing a list of browsers, it indicates which platforms each browser supports or plans to support:

http://browserwatch.iworld.com/

Bookmarks

A particularly important feature of browsers is the **bookmark** that records a document title and URL to enable you to revisit it when you wish to, just as a physical bookmark can take you to a particular page in a book. The bookmark feature on most browsers (occasionally called a **hotlist**) offers a short-cut back to a specific document. This is particularly useful when you find a document purely by chance while browsing the Internet, as it might otherwise be difficult to re-discover the site.

In Netscape, to bookmark the document that you are presently viewing you choose the **Bookmarks** menu option and then **Add Bookmark**. Next time you click on the Bookmarks menu, the bookmark should appear in the list. To re-visit that site in future, all you need to do is click on the name of the document in the bookmark list. In Lynx, use **a** to add a new URL and **v** to view the list.

In Netscape bookmarks can be organized into nested folders, which permits you to create a personal catalogue of useful Internet resources organized in a way that suits you. You can save your bookmarks in order to pass them on to other people, or even use them as the basis for publishing a Web page.

An alternative to bookmarking sites (which is particularly useful if you are not using your own workstation at the time) is to mail the text of documents to yourself or to other people. In Netscape this can be done by using the **Mail Document** command on the **File** menu; you may need to set up details of your e-mail address before you can mail a message – choose the **Options** menu and then select **Mail and News Preferences.**

Common problems

Some problems you may encounter when using Netscape (or another browser) to access the Net include the following messages:

Error 404 means that the document you requested cannot be found on the server. The URL may have been typed in wrongly, or the Web pages may have moved to another server or been removed from the Web altogether. Alternatively, the Web server you are trying to reach may be temporarily inaccessible – it is always worth trying later or the following day.

Server timed out: sometimes error messages are caused when the server you are trying to reach is too busy, and you may receive this message. If this is the case, you should try again at a less busy time (normally mornings and weekends).

If pages take a long time to load, either your local network or one of the networks used to connect to the required site may be busy (this is often described as a **bandwidth** problem), or the remote server may not be able to cope with the number of 'hits' it is receiving. It is always worth switching off the **images** option to speed up the load time, or trying to reconnect at a different time, preferably in the morning.

Sometimes links in pages may have been mistyped by the author of a page – it can be worth trying changing parts of the URL (e.g. substituting lower for upper case, a hyphen for an underscore character or vice versa).

E-mail access

In some cases you may only have limited access to the Internet because of hardware limitations or due to a policy decision on campus. However, it is possible to access almost any Internet resource using e-mail. Simple e-mail commands can be used to access FTP, gopher, Veronica, Usenet, WAIS and the World Wide Web. Even if you do have full Internet access, using e-mail services can save you time and money. However, try to limit your data transfers to one megabyte per day, and don't swamp the servers with many requests at a time.

To retrieve WWW documents by e-mail, all you require is the URL which defines the address of the document, and you can retrieve the text obtained on that page it by sending the message **send URL** (substituting the URL for the site you wish to access for **URL**) to an Agora WWW-mail server (there are several located around the world),

To obtain a document (*The Guide to Offline Internet Access* by Bob Rankin) listing these servers and with full instructions on how to retrieve WWW pages (and other services) by e-mail, send an e-mail message to:

mailbase@mailbase.ac.uk

In the body of your message, enter only this line:

send lis-iis e-access-inet.txt

WWW servers around the world

The number of Web sites is vast and growing rapidly. It would be impossible to list them all. None of the attempts to do so are complete, and you may also need to use the search services described in Chapters 8 and 9 to trace the sites you want.

W3C's *Master Web Server Directory* provides a summary of a list of registered WWW servers. It is available alphabetically by continent, country and state:

http://www.w3.org/pub/DataSources/WWW/Servers.html

The *Virtual Tourist* is a map-based directory of all the WWW servers in the world, created in collaboration with the above list:

http://www.vtourist.com:80/webmap/

For the UK the *United-Kingdom based WWW servers* list at Imperial College is good for academic servers, but less so for commercial ones:

http://src.doc.ic.ac.uk/all-uk.html

The University of Wolverhampton provides two *UK sensitive maps* of WWW servers at universities and colleges and research sites:

http://scitsc.wlv.ac.uk/ukinfo/uk.map.html

Buzz words

The technology of the Web changes rapidly, and here we mention some newer concepts that it is useful to be aware of.

Caching: Anyone who has tried to access a WWW site in North America at 4 pm knows how slow the response time can be because of demand. One technique which helps to improve the response time for WWW end-users and also reduces the network loading is caching. The idea is to enable a local server to keep copies of the Web pages which have recently been browsed. The next time someone else at the same site wishes to access that resource, the browser can retrieve its pages from the cache rather than returning to the source server.

The majority of UK higher-education institutions are now operating caching and there are national ones too.

Java: Java is described by its developers as 'a simple, robust, object-oriented, platform-independent multi-threaded, dynamic general-purpose programming environment'. In plain English this means that it is a computer programming language that has great potential for creating complex applications on the WWW (including animations, simulations and multimedia). Accessing Java applications does require a later version of Netscape or Internet Explorer than may be available on your campus network. Further information on Java can be found at http://sun.java.com/ or http://www.javaworld.com

VRML (or the Virtual Reality Modeling Language) is a develop-ing standard for interactive three-dimensional scenes delivered across the Internet. VRML enables virtual-reality applications to be created, connected by the Internet and hyperlinked with the WWW. Further information on VRML can be found at

http://www.sdsc.edu/vrml

A copy of a FAQ (Frequently Asked Questions – and answers) for the World Wide Web can be found at **http://www.boutell.com/faq/**

File transfer protocol

File transfer protocol, usually abbreviated to FTP, and sometimes known as anonymous FTP, was one of the first uses of the Internet to transfer files between computers. Though other techniques can be used, FTP is still important. It is used much less for text than it once was, because of the ease with which the Web deals with text, but it remains the fastest way of transferring software and images between machines, so you will need to use it to obtain such files for yourself.

Until fairly recently the only way to use FTP was with a separate FTP program, but now a graphical Web browser may do the job more simply. However, we will first outline the older method since that may be all you have access to.

Procedures

For the sake of illustration we will assume you want a file called *raswin.zip* to be found at

ftp://ftp.dcs.ed.ac.uk/pub/rasmol

(this is a URL as described in the previous section).

Using a command line interface

Your central computer system should have an FTP program, usual-ly invoked at the system prompt with **ftp** to give an **FTP>** prompt.

You then enter the address

ftp.dcs.ed.ac.uk

(note that FTP addresses do not always include 'ftp').

You may be able to do all this in one go from the system prompt:

ftp ftp.dcs.ed.ac.uk

If you are connected you will get some sort of response or prompt, so key

login anonymous (hence the name).

You will then be asked for a password, which is your e-mail address (you may be told to enter this). You should then be accepted to the remote machine.

Key **cd pub** to change to the **pub**(lic) directory and **cd rasmol** to change to the **rasmol** directory.

(This is a Unix system, but these commands are similar to DOS commands which you may be familiar with.)

Key **ls -l** to see a list of the files, which will look something like Figure 4.4.

You can thus confirm that the file you want is there, check that the date is correct, and look to see if there are associated files, such as readme and help files you might want. You may also need to note the filesize (e.g. 680780 is the size in bytes) to ensure you have enough filespace available. (These are Unix files, and the d indicates a directory. The rwx etc are file read/write permissions and can be ignored.)

```
-rw-r-xr-x  1 rasmol  local     12703 Nov  2  1994 README
-rw-r-xr-x  1 rasmol  local    952187 Nov  2  1994 RasMol2.tar.Z
-rw-r-xr-x  1 rasmol  local    522691 Oct 28  1994 manual.ps
-rw-r-xr-x  1 rasmol  local   1069808 Oct 28  1994 rasmac.sit.hqx
-rw-r-xr-x  1 rasmol  local    680780 Nov  2  1994 raswin.zip
drwxr-xr-x  2 rasmol  local       512 Oct  9  1995 v2.6beta
-rw-r--r--  1 rasmol  local    398416 Nov 30  1994 vbrun300.dll
```

Fig. 4.4 *A directory of files in a ftp archive*

Key

   get rasmol.zip

and the file should be transferred to your local filespace.

   Repeat this procedure if you need other files.

   If you need to go back up the directory structure use **cd** .. or **cdup**

   When you have finished, key **exit** to go back to your local system prompt.

   Alternatively, if you want to go to another FTP site then key **close** to go back to the **FTP>** prompt and then key the next address.

Using a graphical browser

With a browser like Netscape or a Windows FTP program like WS_FTP or RapidFiler getting files is much easier.

   In Netscape you simply edit the Go To box or use the Open button and key the URL, in this case

   ftp://ftp.dcs.ed.ac.uk/pub/rasmol

(you can include subdirectories).

   Normally Netscape will automate the logon procedure, but occasionally you may need to enter your e-mail address as before.

   Once connected, the list of files is displayed, and you click on the required one, which will be transferred.

   If you are getting files from a software archive such as *Hensa* (mentioned in Chapter 5) then you will not be aware of FTP as you simply find the file and then click on its name to transfer it.

Compression

Many files available by FTP are in a compressed form – that is, they have been processed to reduce their size so as to reduce storage needs and speed up transfer. They then have to be uncompressed after transfer.

   Filenames ending in *.zip* (as in our example), or *.z*, *.tar* or *.zoo* indicate compressed files.

If you are using Netscape to get a file and the appropriate helper applications are configured, then you can decompress the files once they have been retrieved by clicking on **Extract**. If you are using the FTP command you will need to run a decompression program like *PKUNZIP* or WinZip. Such programs may exist on your local system.

If in any doubt about what to do, contact your computing service.

Finding FTP files

You will come across references to FTP files in printed publications and on the Net itself. Usually you will know where to get them but if you have only the name of the file you will need to find a location.

If the file is a program you can try a software archive like *Hensa* or *Sunsite* (see Chapter 6); otherwise use the *Archie* service. Like FTP itself there is the older way of using *Archie* and the simpler way with a graphical browser.

Archie

Archie provides access to an index of files stored in archives across the world. You can search it for a particular filename, or in a very rudimentary way by subject for specific words that might appear in the name or sometimes in a description.

You may have an *Archie* client on your local system – key **archie** to see – but more likely you will have to telnet to a version elsewhere – in the UK the URL is

telnet://archie.doc.ic.ac.uk

and the login is

archie

When connected you will get a prompt:

archie.doc.ic.ac.uk>

There are optional commands at this stage, but the most important is **set pager** which ensures that results are displayed one page at a time.

Key

find *filename*

Searching may take a while – the system usually estimates how long – but eventually you get a list of results showing location, date, directories, filesize and filename (Figure 4.5)

Key

q

if you don't want to page through the whole list.

Note the location/directory/filename details so you can then get the file by FTP. There are likely to be a number of locations, so try the nearest.

Archieplex

Archieplex is the newer way of finding files. Use your Web browser to go to

http://src.doc.ic.ac.uk/archieplexform.html

You then simply fill in a box with the filename, and a list is returned with live links to the archive sites so that you can retrieve the file immediately.

```
Location: /pub/graphics/RasMol/v2.6beta
    FILE   -r-xr-xr-x  364096 bytes  17:21 26 Jan 1996  raswin.exe
    FILE   -r-xr-xr-x  66362 bytes  17:21 26 Jan 1996  raswin.hlp
    FILE   -r-xr-xr-x  304128 bytes  17:21 26 Jan 1996  raswin32.exe
```

Fig. 4.5 *Results of an Archie search*

5

Exclusive to the UK – JANET information services

- ★ BIDS
- ★ FirstSearch
- ★ EDINA
- ★ MIDAS
- ★ AHDS

There are a number of electronic databases and datasets (sets of numerical information) accessible over JANET which are available only to the higher-education community in the UK because they are funded or subsidized by the JISC (the Joint Information Systems Committee – see

http://www/niss.ac.uk/education/jisc/).

The majority of these services require you to register (normally done through your library or computing services, or in some cases online) to obtain a username and password, but are free at point-of-use. This means that you may use them free of charge in connection with your studies since your institution has signed a licence agreement and the subscription will have been paid by your university or directly by JISC. Because you connect over JANET you can use these services from any terminal in your institution that has JANET access. Accessing these services may be your most productive use of the Internet.

> Your university may not subscribe to all those described here – your library will be able to tell you which databases you have access to, and the local arrangements for registering to use them.

The databases described here are similar in function to the printed abstracting journals or CD-ROM services that are available in your library to identify articles and other publications in particular subjects. You may need to consult library staff to decide which of these sources is most appropriate for a specific purpose – in some subjects a printed index may still be best!

The databases provided by *BIDS*, *EDINA*, and *FirstSearch* provide references to journal articles. Many of them have printed equivalents, but you will find that electronic databases can be searched more quickly and allow you to combine search terms in ways which are not possible with printed services. Once you have identified the references, you will then have to check whether your library subscribes to the journals which contain the full text of the articles.

Some of the databases and texts available from *MIDAS* and the *Arts and Humanities Data Service* may be used as raw data in your studies, in conjunction with appropriate software. For example, you may analyse electronic versions of texts by Chaucer obtained from the *Oxford Text Archive*, or use the 1991 Census to discover more about the different types of housing in your area.

BIDS (Bath Information and Data Services)

BIDS is an electronic bibliographic data service for higher education and research, providing access to recent references from journals and conference papers. Several of its databases (including *ISI*, *EMBASE* and *Compendex*Plus*) also include abstracts – a summary of what the article is about.

Databases can be searched for articles of interest using:

★ title words or phrases
★ authors
★ institutional affiliations
★ words in the abstract
★ keywords

or other identifying information.

Bibliographic details can then be displayed on the terminal, or sent to your e-mail account. Remember, these databases do not have the full text of articles. The *BIDS*-hosted databases have a common, simple, easy-to-use, menu-driven interface, with extensive online help screens. *BIDS ISI* and *BIDS BLII* are multi-disciplinary and cover all subject areas, while the other services are more subject-specific.

BIDS services include:

★ *BIDS ISI*: There are three citation indexes (*Science Citation Index*, *Social Science Citation Index* and *Arts & Humanities Citation Index*) containing details of articles drawn from over 7000 journals world-wide from 1981. There is a facility for cited-author searching – that is, looking for recent papers that have referred back to a known relevant paper. Also included is the *Index to Scientific & Technical Proceedings* (ISTP) containing details of papers presented at over 4000 conferences annually.

★ *BIDS BLII*: the British Library's *Inside Information* Service – major articles from 20,000 of the most requested journal titles at the British Library's Document Supply Centre. Coverage begins in 1992.

★ *BIDS IBSS*: the *International Bibliography of the Social Sciences* – a database covering 2600 social-sciences journals world-wide and approximately 6000 books per annum since 1980.

★ *BIDS EMBASE*: *Excerpta Medica Database* – a major pharmacological and biomedical literature database covering 3300 journals from 110 countries from 1980 onwards.

★ *BIDS COMPENDEX*: (Compendex*Plus/Page One): *Engineering Index* database – a major engineering and applied sciences abstracting service covering world wide journals, conference papers and reports since 1978.

★ *BIDS RSC*: seven databases supplied by the Royal Society of Chemistry. Five are bibliographic in nature: *Analytical Abstracts* (from 1979), *Chemical Business NewsBase* (from 1985), *Chemical Engineering & Biotechnology Abstracts* (from 1970), *Chemical Safety NewsBase* (from 1981), and *Mass Spectrometry Bulletin* (from 1991). The remaining databases are *Chemical Safety Data Sheets* (covering 550 chemicals) and the *UK Nutrient Databank* (a database of 60 nutrients in 3000 foods).

★ *UnCover*: a multidisciplinary database of indexed journal articles covering some 15,000 journals. This is freely available through the *BIDS* gateway and a username and password are *not* required.

For further information, help or advice on searching any of the BIDS services, look at their WWW pages

http://www.bids.ac.uk/

or ask your library staff. Full supporting documentation is available for most *BIDS* services, and a *Self-Help* booklet is available for some services, containing many examples of how to use *BIDS* to solve specific problems.

At present access is by telnet to **bids.ac.uk** with a Web version due soon.

Figure 5.1 shows the *BIDS* Gateway screen.

```
|        /
|   BBBB  IIIII  DDDD    SSS
|   B  B    I    D   D   S              Bath Information
|   BBBB    I    D   D   SSS
|   B  B    I    D   D     S            and Data Services
|   B  B    I    D   D   S  S
|   BBBB  IIIII  DDDD    SSS
|   /
| /
|/
          Please type the option letter for the service you require:

   Option   Service                Option   Service
   ------   -------                ------   -------
     I      BIDS ISI                 K      BIDS Kew Record
     B      BIDS BL Inside Information M     BIDS CAB HEALTH
     C      BIDS Compendex/Page One   R      BIDS RSC
     E      BIDS EMBASE               S      BIDS IBSS
     F      BIDS Ecoflora             U      Uncover

     n      News                    q or x  Quit from this gateway
   h or ?   Help
```

Fig. 5.1 *BIDS Gateway screen*

EDINA

EDINA, based at the Edinburgh University Data Library, provides national online services for the UK higher education and research community. These services include:

★ *BIOSIS Previews*: the electronic equivalent of *Biological Abstracts* and *Biological Abstracts/RRM* (Reports, Reviews, Meetings). BIOSIS Previews has comprehensive coverage of international life-science journals and meeting literature.

★ *RAPID: the Research Activities and Publications Information Database* holds information on all research awards (projects, programmes, centres and other activities) supported by the Economic and Social Research Council (ESRC) from April 1985. It also includes details of publications (in the widest sense) that have resulted from ESRC-funded research.

★ *SALSER*: an online information service about periodicals held in Scottish academic and research libraries, including all the university libraries, the National Library of Scotland, Edinburgh City Library, the Mitchell Library in Glasgow, and some union lists.

★ *UKBORDERS*: the online service for extraction of digitized boundary data for the UK. This data can be used for computer-aided mapping of the small area statistics from the 1991 Population Census, mapping 1991 census data systematically at any scale from small area to the whole country, designing new zones from the small area building blocks, and integrating census data fully into geographical information systems.

★ *PCI*: **the** Periodicals Contents Index provides article-level access to the contents of approximately 3500 scholarly journals in the humanities. It includes English-language journals from North America, the United Kingdom and the rest of the English-speaking world, and journals in other European languages including French, German, Italian and Spanish. It focuses on journals published in the twentieth century before 1990.

★ *Palmer's Index to The Times*: Many libraries keep files of *The Times* for historical use. *Palmer's* is the only index to *The Times* for the nineteenth century and is the standard reference work for any library holding the newspaper in printed or microfilm. The online *Index* covers every issue from October 1790 to December 1905 in a comprehensive, cumulative form.

Further information on *EDINA* can be found at:
   http://edina.ed.ac.uk

OCLC *FirstSearch*

FirstSearch from the US company OCLC is an electronic reference service for end-users, consisting of a collection of around 50 electronic bibliographic databases covering books, journal articles, theses, computer software and other types of material. Around one-third of university libraries pay an annual fee to subscribe to a selection of FirstSearch databases.

The databases available include popular commercial databases such as *ERIC*, *Library Literature*, and *Medline*, as well as databases unique to OCLC:

★*WorldCat*: an online union catalogue to many libraries around the world. It contains more than 32 million records describing items on thousands of subjects published since about 1000 AD. Citations include: books, computer data files and programs, maps, manuscripts, musical scores and videotapes.

★*ArticleFirst*: contains details of articles published in nearly 12,500 journals in science, technology, medicine, social science, business, the humanities and popular culture. Coverage is from January 1990.

★*ContentsFirst*: Contains the complete contents pages from individual issues of nearly 12,500 journals in science, technology, medicine, social science, business, the humanities and popular culture. Coverage is from January 1990.

OCLC *FirstSearch* can be accessed by telnet

telnet://fscat.oclc.org/

or via the Web at:

http://www.ref.oclc.org:2000/

An alternative (and sometimes faster) method of access is to go via the *NISS Information Gateway* at:

http://www.niss.ac.uk/datahosts/index.html

Figure 5.2 shows the *FirstSearch* Web page.

MIDAS (Manchester Information Datasets and Associated Services)

MIDAS, a service run by Computing Services, University of Manchester, provides access to a range of national dataset services, such

Fig. 5.2 *FirstSearch screen*

as the 1991 Census of Population Statistics, government and other large continuous surveys, macro-economic time series databanks, digital map datasets, spatial geo-referencing datasets, and scientific datasets.

There is access to software packages and the large-scale computing resources required for data storage, access, manipulation, and analysis/visualization. Software supported by *MIDAS* includes packages for: dataset access/manipulation (such as SASPAC and SPSS), GIS and image processing, crystallographic data processing, and statistical analysis.

Registration forms for the *MIDAS* service can be obtained from your local computing service or via the *MIDAS* WWW site. In order to be able to access a particular dataset, it may be necessary to complete a separate individual registration form to become an authorized user. In some circumstances, access may depend on whether or not your institution has a licence for the service. Information and advice about site and user registration procedures for *MIDAS* and/or particular datasets may be found at

    http://midas.ac.uk/

The *MIDAS* service is at

    telnet://midas.ac.uk

AHDS (Arts and Humanities Data Service)

AHDS is a new initiative which will be offering a range of services to UK higher education in the arts and humanities. It is establishing a small number of service providers, and aims to encourage collaboration among providers of networked information and services, whether commercial or non-profit, in the UK or abroad, in order to promote scholarly use of electronic information in the arts and humanities.

So far three service providers have been designated: *The Oxford Text Archive* (Oxford University Computing Service), the *Historical Data Unit* (The Data Archive, Essex University), and the *Performing Arts Data Service* (PADS) (Glasgow University). They, and others for archaeology and the visual arts, will begin to offer services during 1996 and 1997.

For information on AHDS, see:

http://www.kcl.ac.uk/projects/ahds/top.htm

Help and information for your course work

★ Subject sources – full text, research papers, bibliographies, images, data
★ Specialist sources – electronic journals, newspapers, software, reference, government
★ Library catalogues
★ Teaching and learning material

Though there are a huge number of information sources on the Internet of many types – databases, research reports, numerical and statistical data, images, the text of books and journal articles, newspapers and so on – they still provide only a fraction of the information to be found in the printed books and journals and CD-ROMs that you will have in your library. Nevertheless, Internet sources will grow in importance because of their easy availability, immediacy and multimedia nature.

This chapter gives some guidance as to the sorts of information available, with examples, and directs you to more comprehensive lists online where they exist.

An important source that will be mentioned in various contexts is the *NISS Information Gateway*

http://www.niss.ac.uk

– a government-funded information service for higher education. It has material on the working of education – policy documents and so on from government departments and agencies, higher-education information services, school-performance tables, courses and conferences. It also gathers together much information for day-to-day use, such as:

★ addresses of universities and other institutions
★ research databases and other sources
★ job vacancies
★ reference sources such as dictionaries, e-mail directories, yellow pages, maps
★ financial information
★ electronic newspapers and magazines
★ library catalogues
★ software
★ collections of Internet resources arranged by subject.
★ even TV and radio schedules.

It can often be a useful first place to look.

Types of subject source information

Information sources dealing with specific subjects – such as a bibliography or image of a painting – are vast in number and to list even a representative selection of these for all subjects would be beyond the scope of this book. Here we merely explain what sorts of information you *might* find for your subject and give some examples of these.

> To find what there is for your subjects you will need to browse the subject collections described in Chapter 8. This section can help show you what kind of material to look for.

Text of books

These are sources giving the complete text of out-of-copyright books. They can be viewed online or downloaded to a local file. Some of the material, especially in the humanities, will also be available in printed form, but the electronic version is useful if you want to do any sort of analysis or merely to quote some text in your own work.

You will not normally find student textbooks on the Internet, since publishers still wish to make a living by selling books rather than by offering free information electronically, though there are some pilot projects looking at making recommended texts available in this way.

Oxford Text Archive
http://info.ox.ac.uk/~archive/ota.html
Electronic versions of literary works by many major authors in Greek, Latin, English and a dozen or more other languages.

Encyclopédie, ou Dictionnaire Raisonné des Sciences, des Métiers et des Arts
http://tuna.uchicago.edu/homes/mark/ENC_DEMO
is an online version of the Diderot and d'Alembert encyclopedia published between 1751 and 1772.

Centre for Electronic Texts in the Humanities
http://www.ceth.rutgers.edu

British Poetry 1780-1910: a hypertext archive
http://etext.lib.virginia.edu/britpo.html

Shakespeare Full Text
telnet://lib.dartmouth.edu
then enter
select file shakespeare plays

Victorian (British) Women Writers
http://www.indiana.edu/~letrs/vwwp

Historical text archive
http://www.msstate.edu/Archives/History
World-wide historical material.

Research papers

Accounts of research have normally been published in a journal or conference paper, but increasingly researchers are publishing on the Internet to shorten the time needed to make their work available to other users as well as to widen that availability.

Philosophical Preprint Exchange
http://phil-preprints.L.chiba-u.ac.jp/IPPE.html

Los Alamos E-print Archive
http://xxx.lanl.gov
An archive for new research papers in high-energy physics.

Economics Working Papers Archive
http://econwpa.wustl.edu/Welcome.html
Collects papers from around the world on economic topics for retrieval and discussion.

NetEc
http://netec.mcc.ac.uk/NetEc.html
Bibliography of printed research papers, collection of electronic working papers

Bibliographies and databases

Those databases, like *BIDS* and *FirstSearch*, available to higher education on corporate subscription have been described in Chapter 5, but there are also others, often put together by enthusiasts, which are accessible free of charge. They are likely to cover a fairly limited area, and you will not find them for all subjects. Be aware that their coverage of sources may not be as systematic as databases like *BIDS* or the CD-ROMs produced by commercial and research organizations available in your library, so you may need to use those too for more comprehensive searching.

Hytelnet
http://www.cam.ac.uk/Hytelnet/ful/ful000.html
lists sources available by telnet, and gives access to databases on topics as diverse as Beethoven, Chaucer, East European studies, the Holocaust and mouse genetics.

Poisons Information Database
http://vhp.nus.sg/PID

BLAST
http://www.bio.cam.ac.uk/seqsrch/blast.html
Biological databases on proteins and nucleic acid

CORK
telnet://lib.dartmouth.edu
then enter
select file cork
Databases about alcoholism and substance abuse.

Social Science Research Network
http://www.SSRN.com
A US collection of databases relating to economics, accounting and finance.

Online Bibliography – phonetics and speech technology
http://www.uni-frankfurt.de/~ifb/bib_engl.html

Collection of Computer Science Bibliographies
http://rc.doc.ic.ac.uk/computing/bibliographies/Karlsruhe/index.html

Science Policy Information News
telnet://wisdom.wellcome.ac.uk login: **wisdom**

Internet Movie Database
http://uk.imdb.com

Dictionaries and encyclopaedias

Dictionaries and encyclopaedias on the Internet may merely be versions of those in printed form or may be especially created by taking advantage of the ease of collaboration allowed by the Net.

Dictionary of cell biology
http://www.mblab.gla.ac.uk/~julian/Dict.html
An enhanced version of the printed dictionary published in 1995.

International financial encyclopedia
http://www.euro.net/innovation/Finance_Base/Fin_encyc.html

Online dictionary of computing
http://wombat.doc.ic.ac.uk

Encyclopedia of mythology, folklore, mysticism and more
http://www.webcom.com/myth

Listings of online dictionaries, including foreign-language ones, can be found at
http://www.twics.com/~vladimir/dic.html
and
http://rivendel.com/~ric/resources/dictionary.html

Images – scientific

Much computer data, such as that from space research, may be received as a digital image or used to generate visual interpretations of results. These images can then be made available on the Internet.

NASA
http://www.hq.nasa.gov/office/pao/Library/photo.html
A collection of still images of planets, space vehicles, etc.

Hubble Space Telescope Latest Pictures
http://www.stsci.edu/pubinfo/Latest.html

Images – medical

Similarly medical images may be created from various scanning techniques and may be converted into animated or layered images.

The Visible Human
http://www.nlm.nih.gov/research/visible/visible_human.html
A project to create three-dimensional anatomically detailed representations of the male and female human bodies.

Virtual Frog Dissection
http://george.lbl.gov/vfrog
A three-dimensional representation of the internal structure of a frog with animation and simulation.

Medical Illustrators
http://www.mednexus.com/med_illustrator
Details of illustrators with examples of their work.

Images – historical and artistic

Paintings, drawings and other traditional form of image can be put on the Internet to make them widely and easily available. The image quality is, of course, very poor compared with the original or even with a reproduction in a book.

Dead Sea Scrolls
http://sunsite.unc.edu/expo/deadsea.scrolls.exhibit/intro.html
Images of 100 fragments from the scrolls.

Scottish College of Textiles Gallery
http://www.hw.ac.uk/texWWW/gallery/gallery.html

Louvre
http://mistral.culture.fr/louvre
Images of a variety of artforms from the Louvre Museum.

WebMuseum network
http://sunsite.unc.edu/wm
Covers a wide range of institutions.

Maps

Digital techniques are widely used in mapping, and digital maps
are easily accessed across the Internet. Other maps may simply be
used as a visual way of presenting geographical or locational information. You will also find maps incorporated within Web sites; for
example, to show the plan of a university. Complex maps comprise
large files which may take a long time to download and display. If
you want to reproduce them, you may need a high-resolution printer.

World city maps
**www.lib.utexas.edu/Libs/PCL/Map_collection/Map_collection
.html**

Global Land Information System (GLIS)
telnet://glis.cr.usgs.gov Login: **guest**
Land use maps of the US graphs/data of geological information.

Ordnance Survey
http://www.campus.bt.com/CampusWorld/pub/OS
Includes some maps as well as their catalogue.

The UK and Ireland – an active map
http://www.cs.ucl.ac.uk/misc/uk/intro.html
A map with clickable spots to give photographs and information
on particular towns and cities.

A useful guide to map collections is at
http://www.cgres.uiowa.edu/servers/servers-references.html

Numerical data

Data on the Internet can be valuable because it is likely to be more up to date than in printed sources, particularly for any information that changes regularly, and because wide-ranging sources can be brought together. Being electronic, it can be downloaded and easily reused, perhaps in some modelling or manipulation program. However, the range of data available is still limited compared with printed or charged online sources. Remember there is also the *MIDAS* data service described on page 49.

Scientific

Air Quality Information Service
http://www.aeat.co.uk/products/centres/netcen/airqual/welcome.html
This shows daily levels of air pollutants at various UK locations.

Chip Directory
http://www.xs4all.nl/~ganswijk/chipdir/chipdir.html
has property data for electronic components with links to manufacturers' pages.

Web Elements
http://www.shef.ac.uk/~chem/web-elements/web-elements-home.html
Physical, chemical and biological property data on the chemical elements.

Economic

Electronic Share Information
http://www.esi.co.uk
UK share prices and company information, with many shares updated a number of times a day.

US Bureau of the Census
http://www.census.gov
Includes economic as well as demographic data.

Fortune
http://pathfinder.com/@@50NeCKK4gAIAQCye/fortune/
index.html
Includes searchable databases (Global 500 and Fortune (US) 500
top companies).

Statistical

ESRC Data Archive
http://dawww.essex.ac.uk
Collections of social statistics from UK research. Includes the
BIRON catalogue.

LABSTAT
ftp://stats.bls.gov and http://stats.bls.gov/blshome.html
The US Bureau of Labor Statistics public database, which provides current and historical data from 25 surveys.

Archives catalogues

Leeds Database of Manuscript English Verse
http://www.leeds.ac.uk/library/spcoll/bcmsv/intro.html

Institutional servers

Professional or trade organizations such as the Royal Society of
Chemistry or the Institute of Fiscal Studies usually have a Web presence giving details of their publications, conferences, news, job
vacancies, research activity, members, services, Internet links and so
on. The Web pages for a university department have a similar function.

A collection of such services world-wide is the *Scholarly Societies Project*
http://www.lib.uwaterloo.coc/society/overview.html

Company Web sites

Commercial companies increasingly have Web sites to promote themselves and their products, and often to sell goods across the Internet. They may include some financial or other information about the company which may be useful for academic purposes. Some UK examples of major companies are:

BMW
http://www.bmw.co.uk

Bank of Scotland
http://bankofscotland.co.uk

British Steel
http://www.britishsteel.co.uk

Nationwide Building Society
http://www.nationwide.co.uk

Rolls-Royce
http:/www.rolls-royce.com

You can trace others by using the search services described in Chapter 9.

Interactive – simulation/control

More imaginative uses of the Internet take advantage of its interactive nature by allowing users to input data or requests and responding to them.

The Bradford Robotic Telescope
http://www.telescope.org/rti

Responds to instructions from users on what to look at and provides them with results.

MechanicalGaze
http://vive.cs.berkeley.edu/capek
Allows students to manipulate a camera to view fossils.

Exploratorium
http://www.exploratorium.edu
A collection of electronic exhibits, news and resources for teachers, students and science enthusiasts.

Specialist sources

Electronic journals

There are hundreds of journals, magazines and newsletters published on the Internet. They may look very basic on the screen, having just text, or may be graphically more adventurous with colour and illustrations. Some are the electronic version of a printed journal, but many exist only electronically. Some are newsletters and fanzines (e-zines) produced by enthusiasts; others are reputable academic journals.

Increasingly, established publishers are making available their printed journals to test the Internet as a way of publishing research information more effectively. Access to these may not necessarily be free.

So, for example, Academic Press have 170 journals from 1996 onwards at
http://www.europe.idealibrary.com
and the Institute of Physics provides its journals at
http://www.iop.org
Any user can look at article titles and an abstract, but because of a current higher-education initiative your institution probably has a licence agreement so that you can also view and print the full text of an article. Check with your library about this full text access.

Some other academic publishers such as Chapman & Hall
http://www.chaphall.com/chaphall/journals.html
and the Institution of Electrical Engineers
http://www.iee.org.uk/publish/journals/journals.html
are making their journals available in this way too, but at an additional charge, so not all universities and colleges will have subscribed. Again, check with your library.

To find other electronic journals (or e-journals) there are various lists, of which the most comprehensive is probably the *World Wide Web Virtual Library: Electronic Journals*
http://www.edoc.com/ejournal
which lists nearly 2000. Others are limited to academic titles:

CIC Consortium
http://ejournals.cic.net

University of Pennsylvania
http://www.library.upenn.edu/ej/xej-index.html

Association of Research Libraries
http://www.gold.ac.uk/history/hyperjournal/arl.htm

For the wider range of e-zines try the list maintained by John Labovitz at
http://www.meer.net/~johnl/e-zine-list/index.html
Some journals do not appear in complete form on the Internet, but merely offer extracts from the printed journal as a taster: major articles and features, correspondence, book reviews, jobs and so on. Examples include *New Scientist*
http://www.newscientist.com
Computer Weekly
http://www.computerweekly.co.uk)
and the *Economist*
http://www.economist.com

Tables of contents

At present the number of journals available electronically is only a tiny proportion of those published conventionally, so they can only be used to supplement information from printed journals.

However, the Net can still be used to explore many of these other journals, since there are also services just giving the table of contents (TOC) – that is, article titles, authors and page numbers – of academic journals. You can use these to check the contents of the latest issues of specific journals, or often to search through back issues. You can thus find out about many journals not stocked in your library and may be able also to get an abstract of interesting looking papers to decide whether you want to pursue them further. Some services offer to e-mail you the contents of the latest issue of specified journals.

TOC services include:

Elsevier Science Table of Contents (ESTOC)
http://www.elsevier.com/cas/estoc
Covers 900 journals.

Kluwer
gopher://gopher.wkap.nl
260 journals in the sciences from 1994, which is earlier than most.

MCB University Press
**http://www.mcb.co.uk/services/contents/liblink/webpages/
absindex.html**
130 titles, especially in management.

Oxford University Press
http://www.oup.co.uk/jnls/hdb
60 journals in a range of subjects.

Springer Journals Preview Service
http://www.springer.de/server/svjps.htgml
150 science journals.

Clearly you need to know the publisher to know where to look, and unfortunately not all publishers are included. However, if you have access to services such as *BIDS* and *FirstSearch* (see Chapter 5) then you can use them to get access to the contents pages of thousands of journals.

Software

There is much software available across the Net – indeed, distributing software was one of the earliest uses of the Internet. The subject guides to Internet resources discussed in Chapter 8 include specialist software collections, and the major software companies like Microsoft have Web sites which often include some free software. However, it may be easier to use sources which cover all subjects and for a variety of hardware platforms.

Software available ranges from small utility programs – such as a screen saver, virus checker, HTML editor or decompression program – to large packages such as the Netscape WWW browser, a paint program or a mail system. Although downloading the software is free, some may be 'shareware', that is, you are expected to send the software publisher a small fee to register your use. In return you receive documentation and upgrades. To encourage you to register, the software may become unusable after a prescribed period or a certain date

HENSA Micros

http://micros.hensa.ac.uk

or

telnet://micros.hensa.ac.uk

with username: **hensa** and password: **hensa**) is the microcomputers part of the Higher Education Software Archive – a government funded service. It provides software for a range of computers, including non-DOS machines such as Atari, Mac and Amiga. There is a similar service for Unix software.

SunSITE Northern Europe

http://src.doc.ic.ac.uk

is one of a number of collections world-wide supported by Sun Microsystems, concentrating on programs for PCs and Unix machines.

shareware.com

    http:// www.shareware.com

allows you to search for, browse, and download freeware, shareware, demos, fixes, patches and upgrades from various software archives and computer vendor sites on the Internet

    Software can be downloaded to your computer using FTP as outlined in Chapter 4. The *Archie* service mentioned there can also be used to identify named packages from a much wider range of sources.

    The *NISS Information Gateway* has links to these and other services at

    http://www.niss.ac.uk/it/index.html

Computer documentation

Your local computing service will provide some guidance, support and training for the various services and packages you use, but because of the huge increase in computer use by students in the last few years it may not be able to cope with all the demand. If the documentation provided is inadequate, or you are using software not supported by your institution, you might want to look for documentation elsewhere, since many universities are making theirs available in Web format. You can find a list of such universities at

    http://artws.ucs.ed.ac.uk/Handbook/Catalogues/catalogues.
    html

Some of the sites have a search facility. Remember that if the documentation is written for another university, any logon details will not apply to you.

    You will normally be able to read documentation on the screen, save it into a local file, bookmark it to refer to it later, or print it. However, a variety of formats are used, including PostScript, Word for Windows and Adobe Acrobat files, you will only be able to view these on screen if your browser is equipped to deal with them.

As a supplement to documentation you can use the appropriate newsgroups and discussion lists, particularly the **comp** newsgroups, to ask for help from fellow-users. Chapter 3 suggested some ways of identifying particular lists and newsgroups.

Newspapers and news services

Many newspapers have a presence on the Net. Usually they offer the main UK and world news, business and sports stories of the day. They may also have comment, letters, arts reviews, financial data and the weather. They are, of course, necessarily selective in comparison with the printed newspaper.

Major British electronic newspapers include:

Daily Telegraph
http://www.telegraph.co.uk

Financial Times
http://www.ft.com

Guardian/Observer
http://www.guardian.co.uk

Sunday Times
http://www.sunday-times.co.uk

The Times
http://www.the-times.co.uk

You will need to register for these to get a password. Registration is free and is primarily a marketing exercise.

You can connect to many of these and some US newspapers from the *NISS Information Gateway* at
http://www.niss.ac.uk/news/index.html
European newspapers on the Internet include:

Der Spiegel
http://www.spiegel.de

Die Welt
http://www.welt.de

El Temps
http://www.servicom.es/El_Temps/focus.html

Le Monde
http://www.lemonde.fr

Liberation
http://www.liberation.fr

A comprehensive list of electronic newspapers published throughout the world is maintained by the US *Editor and Publisher* magazine at

http://www.mediainfo.com:4900/ephome/npaper/nphtm/online.htm

There are also news services not based on newspapers like

CNN
http://www.cnn.com

Press Association
http://www.pa.press.net

Reuters
http://www.yahoo.com/headlines/current/international

Content is similar to the newspapers.

Reference

The mixture of reference books you find in your library is beginning to be reflected on the Internet. Here we list a few general sources. Subject-specific ones can be traced from the subject collections described in Chapter 8.

Internet Book Shop
http://www.bookshop.co.uk
is primarily an online book ordering service, but also includes a database of books currently available in the UK. It is thus useful to search for details of books on a particular subject, whether you intend to buy or not.

The commonest dictionary available is *Websters Dictionary*
http://c.gp.cs.cmu.edu:5103/prog/webster
but there is a guide to others at
http://www.bucknell.edu/~rbeard/diction.html

Roget's Thesaurus is at
http://www.thesaurus.com/

Research-It!
http://www.iTools.com/research-it/research-it.html

is a collection of services with a single search page. It includes *Websters Dictionary* and *Roget's Thesaurus*, a quotations dictionary, some language-translation dictionaries, collections of maps, US phone books and US financial information.

CIA World Fact Book is not sensitive information about you or classified military details, but economic, political, geographical etc data about all the countries in the world.
http://www.odci.gov/cia
has a browsable version, or you can search an older version at the *NISS Information Gateway*
http://www.niss.ac.uk/cgi-bin/wrap?wais://wais.niss.ac.uk/World_Factbook.src

YELL
http://www.yell.co.uk
has a lurid yellow colour scheme to suit its name! It has British Telecom services, the Electronic Yellow Pages, a film finder, and a directory of Web sources.

Phone directories
http://www.c2.org/~buttle/tel
contains links to online telephone, fax and business directories from around the world.

You can get weather forecasts from the *Meteorological Office*
http://www.meto.gov.uk
and from the electronic newspapers.

UK Media Internet directory
http://www.whatson.com/ukmedia
has TV, radio, newspaper and magazine addresses and contacts, including e-mail addresses.

Government

Knowledge of what governments are publishing is important not just for those studying the government and politics of the UK, Europe or elsewhere but for all subjects that have to be put into a practical 'real world' context, such as social sciences, business, applied sciences and so on. Only more theoretical subjects like philosophy or mathematics may have little need for government or 'official' information.

You can obtain information from governments world wide on the Net, starting at home with the *Government Information Service* at

http://www.open.gov.uk

This is provided by the CCTA – the UK government's IT division – and contains material from government departments and ministries, agencies like the Building Research Establishment and National Rivers Authority, regulatory bodies, projects such as the Private Finance Initiative, museums and quangos. There is material from local government too.

On this site you will typically find:

★ lists of publications
★ press releases on various developments
★ newsletters

★ programmes of activities
★ service standards and charters
★ explanatory booklets

and other publications which are usually free in their printed version.

You can look at a department's material, browse subject categories like children or disability, or search the full text of the service.

Despite the URL, don't expect too much! The UK government prefers to sell its information, so the content is limited: your library should have a much wider range of government information.

You can use the Internet to find out about recent material your library might have by consulting *NUKOP*

http://www.soton.ac.uk/~nukop

a frequently updated listing of new publications from HMSO, the official government publishers, and from government departments themselves. It is based on the stock of Southampton University Library and covers material published since July 1995.

The European Union has a number of services:

Europa

http://europa.eu.int

has details of EU institutions, speeches, policy documents, statistics and more.

I*M Europe

http://www.echo.lu

is concerned with an information market for Europe, and so has an IT and telecommunications emphasis, but also has details on the European Parliament.

CORDIS

http://www.cordis.lu

is the Community Research and Development Information Service promoting EU R&D activity, with details of projects and publications.

In the USA there is a strong emphasis on freedom of information and open government, recognizing that as the public funds government it is entitled to see the resulting information. So there is *FedWorld*

http://www.fedworld.gov

or

telnet://fedworld.gov

which draws together databases and bulletin boards from 150 agencies. These are useful if you need to examine US practice, but they also have more broadly useful technical and statistical data from bodies such as the Environmental Protection Agency, the Food and Drug Administration and the US Patent Office. There are various databases of publications and a list of government job vacancies.

A comprehensive guide to information sources on government in the US (and elsewhere) is maintained at the University of Texas at

http://www.lib.utexas.edu/Libs/PCL/Government.html

For access to Web servers from national parliaments around the world, try:

http://www.soc.umn.edu/~sssmith/Parliaments.html

Library catalogues

The most important source of local information will be the catalogue of your own library. Computer-based library catalogues are often referred to as OPACs (Online Public Access Catalogues), and an increasing number have Web interfaces too. Your own catalogue is likely to be available locally on your campus network.

Always check how much of the library's stock is available on the OPAC – some long-established university libraries do not list their earlier books on the OPAC, and you may have to refer to a card or microfiche catalogue to check on older material. Most catalogues will also list the periodicals taken.

The Internet will allow you to search other OPACs from your own institution. There are various reasons why you might wish to do this:

★ to check for books and journals from another local academic library. Usually a university or college library will allow students from other local institutions to consult or photocopy material, though some may limit access during term time. Your own library will advise on what facilities are available, or you may be able to find this information on the WWW pages of the institution whose library you plan to visit.

★ to check a library you wish to use elsewhere in the country, for example, during vacations or on placement.

★ to search the catalogue of a library that specializes in a topic that you are studying, in order to identify useful sources. For example, if you are studying American or Australian literature, you might wish to search the OPACs of the Library of Congress or the National Library of Australia.

★ to search major copyright libraries which receive copies of all new books published in the UK.

Please note that if you locate books in other libraries which you wish to borrow, your library will normally borrow them through the British Library's Document Supply Centre, rather than going directly to the library whose OPAC you have searched.

The *NISS Information Gateway*

http://www.niss.ac.uk/reference/opacs.html

provides access to most British academic library catalogues, in addition to some in other countries. Do check the **[Info]** box before connecting to an OPAC, as it often contains useful information on the coverage of the OPAC and how to log off from the service – it is sometimes easy to get stranded without knowing how to log off.

COPAC

http://copac.ac.uk/copac/

marks the beginning of a 'national OPAC' service based on the union catalogue database of the Consortium of University Research Libraries (CURL). COPAC currently gives access to the combined university library catalogues of Cambridge, Edinburgh, Glasgow, Leeds and Oxford Universities, and the catalogues of a further ten

CURL member libraries will be added. The service provides search, retrieve, display and download facilities, and is under development. Access to COPAC is free of charge.

Another listing of UK catalogues – and, more importantly, those from the USA and other countries – is the *Hytelnet* service . This gives access details of catalogues, and also allows telnet access to them and to databases and other services too.

Hytelnet can be accessed in a Web version at the University of Cambridge at:

http://www.cam.ac.uk/Hytelnet/

or by telnet to Oxford University at

telnet://rsl.ox.ac.uk (log in as hytelnet).

Teaching and learning material

As we have seen, much of the material on the Internet is of value for learning purposes, particularly in providing facts, information, opinions and so on. However, there is also course material with a specifically educational role that gives a structured and guided view of a topic, comprising all or some of the following:

★ lecture notes
★ case studies
★ illustrations
★ video clips
★ simulation
★ animation
★ tests
★ assignments
★ support by e-mail
★ links to useful information.

Some courses are offered to anyone who wishes to sign up; others are designed for specific institutions, but can be used by others. It is possible that your own course may use something specially prepared in this way – for all or part of a unit/module – or that you will be referred to some other college's online course, but it is more likely that you will simply want to look around to see if there is anything that could be used to supplement your own course material. You might find useful background information, such as guidance on using particular computer systems or software, or you may prefer the self-paced learning possible with computer-based material.

There are collections of such material which arrange them in broad subject areas and have some description of the content. The largest of these is the *World Lecture Hall* at the University of Texas

    http://www.utexas.edu/world/lecture/index.html

and there is a similar one – *Teaching and learning on the Web* – at Maricopa Community College

    http://www.mcli.dist.maricopa.edu

The subject collections described in Chapter 8 will include this sort of teaching material.

Most of these courses are from the USA, so they are not always relevant to the UK context, and transatlantic network congestion can sometimes make their use slow and frustrating.

A UK source you might look at is BT's *CampusWorld*

    http://www.campus.bt.com/CampusWorld/pub/index.html

Though intended mainly for schools, its content is growing in relevance for college students.

7

Finding jobs, loans and more . . .

★ Grants/loans
★ Placements/studying overseas
★ Travel
★ Jobs
★ Counselling/support

As a student you may need information for purposes other than assignments and course work, so this chapter suggests some sources to help with placements, job hunting and so on. A general source you might try is *Student Pages on the Web*

http://www.studentpages.com/

which has local information, careers details, competitions and links to universities, newspapers and other Internet resources.

Grants/loans

Student grants and loans: a brief guide for higher education students 1996/97

http://www.open.gov.uk/dfee/loans/loans.htm

is the document from the Department for Education and Employment which you may have in its printed form.

The *Student Loans Company*

http://www.slc.co.uk

has information on loan terms, eligibility, repayments, how to apply and so on. You cannot yet apply through the Internet!

Placements

Many courses include a period of placement, varying from a few weeks to a year. Departments are often well organized about recommending suitable placements, but sometimes you will have to find your own. Usually it is necessary to use a directory of companies and organizations for your subject, perhaps with a geographical breakdown. There are not yet many trade directories of this sort on the Internet, but useful ones include:

Freepages

http://www.freepages.co.uk

which claims to be the biggest classified UK business directory on the WWW, with 1.6 million entries.

YELL: Electronic Yellow Pages

http://www.yell.co.uk/yell/eyp.html

is an electronic version of BT's *Yellow Pages*, listing contact details of 1.6 million UK businesses. It is searchable by location and category.

Europages: the European business directory

http://www.europages.com

has details of 150,000 suppliers from 25 countries. You can search the database by keyword or company name. Contact details and brief business descriptions are given.

Yellow pages online

http://www.ypo com

has contact details of 18 million US companies, searchable by industry, name, brand name.

These directories won't provide much information about the companies, so you may still need to consult printed trade directories or CD-ROM services such as *FAME* in your library.

Overseas study

Alternatively you may be spending a term/semester/year in another country. The institution to which you are going will doubtless have a WWW server from which you can get information about it. You can check for it on the world list of Web servers at

http://www.w3.org/hypertext/DataSources/WWW/Servers.html

or maybe find the URL more easily with one of the search services discussed in Chapter 9.

If you want information on the country you are going to then you can try *The Virtual Tourist*

http://www.vtourist.com/vt

or the *CIA World Fact Book* at

http://www.odci.gov/cia

for the latest edition or

http://www.niss.ac.uk/cgi-bin/wrap?wais://wais.niss.ac.uk/World_Factbook.src

to search an earlier one.

Remember that when you are on placement or studying elsewhere you may have access to e-mail to keep in touch with your university or college.

Travel

The Net is a suitable medium to distribute the continually changing information on travel – fares and timetables – and soon you will also be able to book seats using it. Some useful sources are:

Campus Travel
http://www.campustravel.co.uk/campus.htm
offers flights, ground transport and insurance worldwide.

Internet world travel guide
http://www.iwtg.com
deals with a variety of means of travel.

UK Railways on the Net
http://www.rail.co.uk
provides information from the numerous new UK railway companies.

RailServer
http://rail.rz.uni-karlsruhe.de/rail/english.html
is a database of about 28,000 stations all over Europe, with complete timetable information for Germany and a selection of trains for other countries.

Jobs

The Internet is becoming an important source of information on job vacancies, sometimes to supplement advertisements in the newspapers and magazines, but increasingly as the only place where vacancies are announced. The recruitment process is quicker, and there are even cases of people being interviewed for overseas jobs by e-mail!

Initially these services were concerned largely with jobs in IT, but increasingly they cover a wider range of jobs, though outside the academic area these are mostly in management and finance. They may advertise vacancies or allow you to submit a CV for recruiters to consider.

The *NISS Information Gateway*
http://www.niss.ac.uk/noticeboard/index.html
maintains lists of vacancies in higher education arranged by subject and also has jobs from publications like the *New Scientist*, *The Times* and *The Guardian*, and from various other sources. It also links to some of the services noted below.

The Central Services Unit, which publishes UK job vacancies in printed form, also has a Web site called *ProspectsWeb*
http://www.prospects.csu.man.ac.uk
with details of vacancies, postgraduate courses and potential employers.

Other sources for student opportunities are Graduate Horizons
http://www.ivision.co.uk/arcadia/horizons
and *Gradunet, the On-Line Graduate Recruitment Guide*
http://www.gradunet.co.uk
There are a number of general UK recruitment agencies with a Web presence, such as:

Executive Class
http://ourworld.compuserve.com/homepages/execlass/
for professional and executive recruitment.

Reed Employment
http://www.reed.co.uk

People Bank
http://www.peoplebank.com

Top Jobs on the Net
http://www.torres.co.uk

and others that specialize in particular areas, such as:

Chadwick Nott
http://www.careerpoint.co.uk
for law and accountancy.

IT Jobs Homepage
http://Internet-Solutions.com/itjobs.htm
with links to many IT recruitment agencies.

Job Serve
http://www.jobserve.com for IT.

O'Connell Associates
http://www.oconnell.co.uk
for financial services.

4Schools Jobnet
http://www.worldserver.pipex.com/c4schools/jobnet/index.html
for teaching and other educational vacancies.

You can also find out about jobs on discussion lists:
On *Mailbase* there are **gis-jobs and immunology-vacancies**
There are numerous US-based lists that have vacancies, but naturally with a US bias. If you need to find them try searching *Liszt*
http://www.liszt.com
a collection of 50,000 lists.

Relevant Usenet groups include:

alt.jobs; bionet.jobs.offered; bionet.jobs.wanted; biz.jobs.offered; uk.jobs.offered and uk.jobs.wanted

The newspaper services mentioned in Chapter 6 also include job advertisements.

Counselling and support

If you have personal, financial, health or other problems affecting your work there are many people to talk to, for example tutors, lecturers, friends, student counsellors, chaplains and so on. However, if you find it easier to communicate less directly then you may be able to find appropriate help on the Internet.

The Samaritans can be found at

http://www.compulink.co.uk/~careware/samaritans

If you have access to Usenet then there are numerous newsgroups in the **alt.support** hierarchy dealing with topics such as diet, depression, loneliness, learning disabilities and various medical problems.

There is a useful guide called *Emotional support on the Internet* that lists pertinent newsgroups and discussion lists. It is issued regularly on many relevant newsgroups as a FAQ and is available at:

http://www.lib.ox.ac.uk/internet/news/faq/archive/support. emotional.resourceslist.html

You might find the National Union of Students site at

http://www.nus.org.uk

helpful.

Student newspapers

Student newspapers are beginning to appear on the Web. Some examples are:

Courier at the University of Newcastle
http://www.ncl.ac.uk/~ncourier

Epigram at Bristol University
http://www.bris.ac.uk/Depts/Union/Epigram/welcome.htm

Student at Edinburgh University
http://www.ed.ac.uk/~eusn/contents.html

8

Tips on browsing for subject information

★ Subject resource guides
★ Multidisciplinary subject collections without annotations
★ Multidisciplinary subject collections with annotations
★ Subject gateways

There are two main ways to track information on the Internet: searching using a search engine or other retrieval tool (see Chapter 9), or browsing in an Internet subject directory or virtual library, which this chapter deals with. Here we discuss a number of projects and services which have been set up in response to the need for better subject access to Internet resources.

The earliest collections of resources organized by subject were known as **subject trees**, which were originally gopher-based. Subject trees offer a method of organizing related resources without regard to their physical location, and normally include direct links to the listed resources. Nowadays they are more frequently referred to as subject collections or **subject gateways**, and may either be multidisciplinary or focus on a particular subject area. They are ideally suited to browsing for information, when you wish to know what resources are available in a specific discipline or subject area.

Subject resource guides

There have been many guides created which list the full range of Internet resources (WWW, gophers, discussion lists, newsgroups, FTP archives, etc) in particular subject areas. If a guide has been produced for a topic of interest to you, then much of the preliminary browsing has already been done for you – provided that the guide is comprehensive and is kept up-to-date!

The major collection of these guides is the *Argus Clearinghouse*
http://www.clearinghouse.net/
(formerly known as the Clearinghouse for Subject-Oriented Internet Resource Guides). Unfortunately, guides are not available for every subject area and in some cases are merely lists of discussion lists. One useful feature of the Clearinghouse is that it provides the date on which a guide was last updated and contact details for the author.

Multidisciplinary subject collections

The *World Wide Web Virtual Library* at CERN was the first subject-based collection of WWW resources, predating the development of graphical Web browsers. It is created by volunteers from around the world, who are often experts in their own field. The general URL is
http://www.w3.org/pub/DataSources/bySubject/Overview.html
but you will find that specific subject sections are based wherever they are maintained.

Within the UK, two of the earliest projects which collected and organized Internet resources are the *BUBL Subject Tree*
http://www.bubl.bath.ac.uk/BUBL/cattree.html
and the *NISS Directory of Network Resources.*
http://www.niss.ac.uk/subject/index.html
The *BUBL Subject Tree* has alternative approaches – subjects are listed in alphabetical order and by the UDC library classification. NISS's *Directory* is selective in the resources it includes – they are primarily UK information sources available on the JANET network that might be of interest to the UK academic community. It

provides a description of all Internet resources included in the *Directory* – click on the link marked **[Info]** next to any resource listed. *BUBL* is developing a new service known as *LINK* (LIbraries of Networked Knowledge) to replace the Subject Tree.

The *Wolverhampton Web Library*

http://www.scit.wlv.ac.uk/wwlib/newclass.html

is a searchable classified catalogue of UK Web pages. The catalogue is organized using Dewey Decimal Classification, and seeks to be comprehensive in its coverage of UK sites, while also including non-UK pages of multinational organizations active in the UK.

Galaxy and *Yahoo* provide subject access to the Internet, but without any description or review of the resources listed. Both include a search facility (searching the URL, headings, description), and Boolean searching (described in Chapter 9). In addition, *Galaxy* ranks the results of a search by score.

Galaxy

http://www.einet.net/galaxy.html

provides 11 main subject categories, each of which includes up to 40 sub-headings to browse: Business and Commerce, Community, Engineering and Technology, Government, Humanities, Law, Leisure and Recreation, Medicine, Reference, Science, and Social Sciences.

Yahoo

http://www., ahoo.com/

is frequently talked about as a search tool, but it is more accurately described as a virtual library or catalogue and is probably the largest subject collection. Users can search the database or browse down *Yahoo*'s fourteen hierarchical categories: Arts, Business and Economy, Computers and Internet, Education, Entertainment, Government, Health, News, Recreation and Sports, Reference, Regional, Science, Social Science, and Society and Culture. Yahoo are launching a range of country-specific Yahoo databases, including *Yahoo UK and Ireland*

http://www.yahoo.co.uk

Another important, though selective, listing of Internet resources, which can provide a useful starting point for browsing, is Scott

Yanoff's *Special Internet Connections*
  http://www.spectracom.com/islist/
This is organized by subject and updated twice a month.

Multi-disciplinary subject collections with annotations

An increasing number of Internet sites include icons which indicate
that they have been given an award. During 1995 and 1996 there
has been a growth in Web services such as Magellan and Point (see
below) which describe themselves as 'review' sites. These services
have created databases of resources which have been selected (and
sometimes reviewed or evaluated) according to particular criteria.
However, sometimes criteria like design and 'coolness' may take
precedence over information content. Most include a search facility
in addition to the opportunity to browse by subject.
  Excite
  http://www.excite.com
is primarily a large database of Internet resources, which offers two
approaches to locating information: NetSearch and NetReviews.
NetSearch searches every record in the database, but NetReviews filters resources and does not include sites which fail to provide 'any
significant quantity of information on any topic'. NetReviews has
been likened to a library catalogue, in that it points to Web sites
(rather than pages) and Usenet groups (rather than individual articles) just as a catalogue leads to a book rather than pages or chapters.
NetReviews is organized by topic in a many-tiered hierarchy. To use
Excite's NetReviews to its full potential, it is important to read the
site's *Handbook* which discusses classification, search strategies,
Boolean syntax, and relevance indicators.
  Magellan
  http://www.mckinley.com/
(also known as the McKinley Internet Directory) is an online directory of described, rated and reviewed Internet resources. It presents
both ratings and detailed previews of descriptions at the first level of
searching. A powerful full-text search engine allows users to refine

their searches further, and Magellan offers a range of search operators in its Advanced Search mode. The subject categories are hotlinked to provide additional resource selections. Magellan operates within clearly defined editorial guidelines and does not include sites that promote pornography, paedophilia or hatred.

NetFirst

http://www.oclc.org/oclc/netfirst/

is a database of Internet resources produced by OCLC Inc. It has been designed as an authoritative index, containing enough information to enable users to evaluate the relevance of a resource before they connect to it. Resources are not selected or excluded on the basis of subject matter, as it is the quality of the data which is the primary criterion. However, records are classified by subject, and users can restrict or enable access. NetFirst contains approximately 45,000 records, providing extensive coverage of Web sites, Usenet newsgroups, discussion lists, and anonymous ftp sites.

The NetFirst database is available at

http://www.netfirst.ac.uk/

free of charge to staff and students at UK higher education institutions. In order to access the NISS NetFirst Service you will need an account name and password issued by your NISS Site Administrator – ask staff in your library or computing service for details.

Point Web Reviews

http://www.pointcom.com/

give descriptions and ratings to all Web sites included in their 'Top 5%'. Point staff claim that excellence is their only criterion, and make no distinction between commercial, private or student pages. Point's rating scale ranges from 0 to 50, scoring in three categories (content, presentation, and experience).

WebCrawler Select

http://152.163.202.23/select/

(formerly known as *GNN Select* and the *Whole Internet Catalog Select*) includes brief reviews of sites. Described as a 'hand-picked collection of the best sites the Internet has to offer', it includes only sites which have been reviewed and organized into 'surfable subject categories': Arts and Entertainment, Business, Computers, Daily News, Education, Government and Politics, Health and Medicine, Humanities, Internet, Life and Culture, Personal Finance, Recreation and Hobbies, Science and Technology, Sports and Travel.

Table 8.1 summarizes the types of Internet resource included by the multi-disciplinary subject collections

Table 8.1   Types of Internet resource included by the multi-disciplinary subject collections

Name of service	WWW	gopher	telnet	ftp	newsgroups	discussion lists
BUBL Subject Tree	Yes	Yes	Yes	Yes	No	No
Excite	Yes	No	No	No	Yes	No
Galaxy	Yes	Yes	Yes	No	No	No
Magellan	Yes	Yes	Yes	Yes	Yes	No
NetFirst	Yes	Yes	Yes	Yes	Yes	Yes
NISS Directory of Network Resources	Yes	Yes	Yes	Yes	No	No
Point Web Reviews	Yes	No	No	No	No	No
WebCrawler Select	Yes	No	No	No	No	No
WWW Virtual Library	Yes	No	No	No	No	No
Wolverhampton Web Library	Yes	No	No	No	No	No
Yahoo	Yes	Yes	Yes	Yes	Yes	Yes
Yanoff's Special Internet Connections	Yes	Yes	Yes	Yes	Yes	No

Subject gateways

Some projects, often known as subject gateways, choose to collect and evaluate Internet resources in a particular subject area. Some of these have been collected together as part of the *World Wide Web Virtual Library* (see page 85). In the UK, a group of subject gateways is being funded through **eLib**, the Electronic Libraries Programme; these can be accessed as a group at:

http://ukoln.bath.ac.uk/elib/lists/anr.html

ADAM (art, design, architecture and media)
http://adam.ac.uk/

CAIN (conflict studies)
http://www.ulst.ac.uk/cain/index.htm

biz/ed (economics and business)
http://www.bizednet.bris.ac.uk:8080

EEVL (engineering)
http://eevl.ac.uk/

IHR-Info (History)
http://ihr.sas.ac.uk/ihr/ihr0101.html

OMNI (biomedicine)
http://omni.ac.uk/

RUDI (urban design)
http://rudi.herts.ac.uk/

SOSIG (social science)
http://sosig.ac.uk/

The majority of these gateways will follow the structure of SOSIG, the most established and highly-developed of these projects, and will provide a comprehensive list of relevant UK-based sources in their subject area as well as a guide to high-quality international resources. All the resources that appear on the gateway meet specific selection criteria and will have been catalogued and described. In many cases the resource descriptions may be browsed before connecting directly to the resource itself. A search facility, allowing keyword searching of the descriptions and other information, will also be available. Some eLib-funded subject gateways will not go live until late 1996.

Four other UK-based sites which may be regarded as subject gateways are:

HUMBUL

http://info.ox.ac.uk/departments/humanities/international.html
which acts as an international gateway for the humanities, listing subject-specific resources in: Anthropology; Archaeology; Classics;

Electronic Text Centres, Text Archives, and Literature; Film, Drama, and Media Studies; History; Hypermedia and Multimedia; Language and Linguistics; Mediaeval Studies; Music; Philosophy; Religious Studies, and the Visual Arts, Art History, Museums and Exhibitions.

Business Information Sources on the Internet
http://www.dis.strath.ac.uk/business/index.html
(Sheila Webber) is a selective guide to Internet sites which contain business information, with some emphasis on UK sources.

Chemdex
http://www/shef.ac.uk/~chem/chemdex/
is an extensive collection of chemistry-related Internet resources, including *WebElements*, the Periodical Table database on the WWW.

PICK
http://www.aber.ac.uk/~tplwww/e/
aims to facilitate access to electronic materials in the field of library and information science.

Further information on subject searching

John December provides two commentaries on subject-oriented browsing on the Internet, with links to many services, as part of his *CMC Information Sources*
http://www.december.com/cmc/info/internet-searching-subjects.html
and *Internet Web Text*:
http://www.december.com/web/text/nar-subject.html

Finally, do not rule out 'serendipity' – the art of discovering valuable information by accident. Many important academic discoveries have been made in this way, and even experienced Internet searchers claim 'serendipity' as a defence for spending time 'net-surfing'! Using the resources and tools discussed in this and the following chapter should cut down on the time you spend browsing and searching for information, and so give you more time to make serendipitous discoveries.

9

Tips on searching for information

★ Boolean and other concepts for searching
★ World Wide Web search tools
★ Searching discussion lists and newsgroup message archives
★ Using Veronica to search gopher resources
★ Search tool collections

The previous chapter discussed various subject collections of Internet resources, and often these will be the first place to look when you are unsure where to find some information. The other way to locate information is to use various services that search the text of World Wide Web files, gopher menus or e-mail archives. In addition, as has been noted in previous chapters, you can search particular resources such as an e-mail directory, a large text file, databases like those from *BIDS*, FAQs, an archive like *Archie* and sometimes the content of specific Websites, such as the *NISS Information Gateway* or many university Web services. (Some of these may use a method called WAIS – Wide Area Information Server – to search text, but you will not usually need to know much detail about using that). This chapter concentrates on the more general services that find textual information.

Concepts

To use any of these search facilities you need to understand some of the concepts used. You may be familiar with some of these if you have searched CD-ROMs in your library.

Boolean logic

Of most importance is the use of AND, OR and NOT (Boolean logic).

★ Use AND to join concepts to make a search more specific. You want *all* the words to be present, e.g. **oil AND pollution AND north AND sea**

★ Use OR to widen the search when you want *any* of a set of words to be present, or to specify synonyms, e.g. **marine OR ocean OR sea**

★ Use NOT to *exclude* words, e.g. **pollution NOT air**

You can create more complex searches by using brackets, e.g. **oil AND pollution AND (sea OR ocean OR marine)**

Some search services may ask you to enter search terms (or **key-words**) in a box without making clear whether it will use AND or OR in searching, so you need to find out first. Some services require you to type AND or OR, others to check a box to indicate which you want. Some use + or − as alternative commands.

Search tips

The ability to search on part of a word so as to find material on similar words can simplify searching. So **medic** (maybe input as **medic%, medic?** or **medic***) will find material containing 'medical' or 'medicine'. This process is known as truncation, word stemming or using a wildcard.

For large databases or textual material it is useful if you can restrict your search to a particular part (or field) of the information on the database, such as the document title, the summary (or abstract), index terms, or the URL for Internet resources, so as to get more accurate results. So if you are just trying to find a URL for a particular organization, for example, limiting the search on the organization's name to the URL field should give a more rapid result.

Many services use a scoring mechanism based on the placing of the keywords and their frequency, assuming that a document will be more relevant if the words appear in its title or frequently throughout the pages rather than occuring once at the end of the document. The results of your search will be displayed with the highest scoring first – maybe showing a numerical value with a maximum of 1.0, 1000 or 100%. This process is not always effective, however, so do not assume that only the first 10 or 20 sources retrieved will be of value. You may need to look further through the list.

Many services are searching very large databases – those for the Web are looking through millions of pages – so any words you look for may appear thousands of times. While a search for an uncommon name would probably find a small number of useful items, it is not a good idea to look for a single common name such as 'AIDS' without being more precise unless you are willing to plough through thousands of references. You would also usually find references containing the word 'aids'.

The context of the words you want may be wrong too, so a search for 'John Major' or 'John AND Major' might find Major John somebody or a document that refers to, say, Clancy Major and John someone else. However, some services do include a NEAR command to find words that are close together, and some allow you to search for phrases.

Don't forget to consider alternative words or phrases. Thus, if you wanted to find out about fibre optics (used for computer and telephone network cables), you would need to take account of the US spelling 'fiber' and the phrase 'optical fibres' which is also used.

So, though most search services simply encourage users to enter a word or words, you can see that it is important to have a little knowledge of how they work and the search options they offer. First you need to think about your subject and decide on the words (including synonyms) that you will use, and how to link them with Boolean commands. Then, when using a service, you should read the instructions carefully before entering your search terms – these may be on the search screen, or you may have to look for a 'help', 'info', 'about', 'tips' or 'instructions' option that calls up detailed guidance, maybe with examples. Unfortunately you cannot assume that because you know how to use one service you can use the others – each Web search service in particular has its own way of doing things!

World Wide Web search tools

Web search tools (alternatively called search programs, search services or search engines) are usually promoted as the only way to find information on the Internet, but, of course, the Web is only part of the Internet, albeit the dominant one. These tools cannot search services available only by telnet, ftp archives, or message archives and most do not include gopher sources, but may include Usenet groups and e-mail address directories. There are many different Web search services, searching different parts of the Web in different ways, and you have only to do a simple search using three or four of them to see that they can produce quite different results for the same subject, so you need to understand something about how they work.

The World Wide Web is an unstructured and ever changing collection of information so there is no clearly defined 'Web' for these services to search. They each create their own version of the Web by using 'robot' or 'crawler' programs. These start from a basic list of Web sources and follow the hyperlinks to other sources, recording details of the pages they find into a database. Different starting-points and robots that work in different ways, mean that the databases created will be different in content. Similarly there may be differences in the way these databases are indexed and searched. This explains why search services do not give the same results in response to a given search request. It is thus important to look at any help files to see how they work and how to use them.

Examples

There are many different search services, and new ones appear regularly, usually claiming to be bigger, faster and more effective than existing ones, and often displacing them in popularity. At present the most useful ones are:

Alta Vista
http://www.altavista.digital.com

Excite
http://www.excite.com

Infoseek
http://www2.infoseek.com

Infoseek Ultra
http://ultra.infoseek.com

Inktomi
http://inktomi.berkeley.edu

Lycos
http://lycos.cs.cmu.edu

Open Text
http://index.opentext.net

WebCrawler
http://webcrawler.com

Their key features are shown in Table 9.1

Table 9.1 Features of Internet search services

	Other sources	Implied OR	Using + and –	Uses AND,OR, NOT	Specify fields to search	Truncation	Adjacency	Proximity
Alta Vista	Usenet	Yes	Yes	In Advanced Search	Yes	Uses *	Uses " "	Uses NEAR
Excite	Usenet	See note	Yes	Yes	No	No	No	No
Infoseek	Usenet E-mail addresses	Yes	Yes	No	No	No	Uses " "	Uses [ ]
Infoseek Ultra	No	Yes	Yes	Yes	Yes	No	Uses " " or ADJ	No
Inktomi	No	See note	Yes	No	No common endings	Strips	No	No
Lycos	No	Yes	No	Yes	No	Treats term as a word stem	No	No
Open Text	Usenet	No	No	Yes	Yes	No	Assumes a phrase	Uses NEAR
Web-Crawler	No	Yes	No	Yes	No	No	Uses " "	Uses NEAR

Notes:

'Other sources'. The service may search other Internet sources as well as the World Wide Web pages: most commonly the message archives of Usenet newsgroups.

'Implied OR'. A user keys in words relating to the topic required and the system will look for any of them. However, *Excite*, Inktomi and *Infoseek Ultra* take account of when more than one of the words are present and when displaying results those with all the requested terms are listed first.

'Using + and –'. Terms that must be present can be prefixed with + (the 'require' symbol). Those that must not be present can be indicated with – ('reject')

'Adjacency'. Specify that words must be next to each other, as in a phrase or person's name.

'Proximity'. Ensure that search words are near each other, e.g. in the same sentence or within a certain number of words.

There is no 'best' search service, though at the time of writing *Alta Vista* probably has the largest database and *Infoseek Ultra* is the fastest. You may find you prefer one or two over the others, especially if you just want 'something' on a subject, or if you need to use a particular search feature, but for an effective search – to find a very precise piece of information or to find as much as possible – you may need to use a number of them.

There are also services that search all of these from one search screen (sometimes known as 'meta-search' services) so that you can avoid having to connect to lots of them. The best of these is *Metacrawler*

http://metacrawler.cs.washington.edu:8080

However, this returns only the first 10 items from each service and the common search screen means you do not have the flexibility of using different search methods offered by the individual services.

These Web search services are all US-based, and though they do have a world-wide coverage they tend to be dominated by US sources. If you want a more limited coverage geographically – e.g. to find the URL for a German university, or information that must relate to Britain – then try the following:

For the UK: *GOD (Global Online Directory)*

http://www.god.co.uk

For Europe: *EuroFerret*

http://www.muscat.co.uk

Newsgroups and discussion lists

Though discussion-list and newsgroup messages might seem ephemeral, they are normally stored for a while, and can be a valuable source of up-to-date practical information and news. There are various ways to search archives for many of these, though unfortunately not for all discussion lists.

The UK *Mailbase* service

http://www.mailbase.ac.uk/

keeps 12 months' messages for each of its lists. These can be browsed or searched, though only for each list and not collectively. The archives use the Hypermail program to allow connection to any Internet sources quoted in messages. Extensive documentation is available.

Lists using the *Listserv* mailing program allow a batch search of archives – that is, you send a message with your search requirement and receive an e-mail response. When you join such a list you will receive instructions on searching.

A small number of lists have set up searchable databases of messages, either as a telnet or as a Web site, and again you will be informed if this is so when you subscribe.

The archives of newsgroups can be searched in various ways. *DejaNews*

http://www.dejanews.com/

claims to be the largest collection of indexed Usenet newsgroups and includes messages since March 1995. It offers extensive query filters.

A Usenet option is also offered by a number of the Web search services discussed in the previous section (see Table 9.1). They have different search facilities, and you need to check their 'help' files to see how much of Usenet is covered and how far back they search.

Searching gopherspace

Though gopher is not used much these days for new services, a great deal of information remains available on gopher servers around the world, particularly on university systems. The search program for gophers is called **Veronica**, supposedly standing for Very Easy Rodent-Oriented Net-wide Index of Computerized Archives, where the 'rodent' is a gopher. Veronica searches by keyword only in the titles of documents, rather than in the full text (like many Web search services), but these documents may contain images or sound files. A simple query on Veronica will consist of one or more keywords, and more complex searches can include the use of Boolean terms. The symbol * is used for truncation, at the end of a word.

Veronica is offered as an option on most gopher servers, but if your institution does not run a gopher server any more, try the extensive list accessible on the *BUBL Information Service* at gopher://ukoln.bath.ac.uk:7070/11/Type/Gophers

A FAQ explaining Veronica is available at:

gopher://gopher.scs.unr.edu:70/00/veronica/veronica-faq

Search tool collections

There are various collections of search services you can use that can make it easier to remember what is available. They usually link to Web search services and e-mail address directories, and maybe to subject collections and 'what's new' services too. Sometimes, however, they are just long lists that may confuse you, and they often give insufficient guidance on the use of services.

Graphical browsers used to access the Web usually have a search option like Netscape's 'Net Search' button that links to the search services noted here and usually to others too.

The UK *BUBL Information Service* has a list of services that also includes links to some studies of the value of different ones

http://www.ukoln.ac.uk/BUBL/Key.html

A good selective collection is the *Scout Toolkit*

http://rs.internic.net/scout/toolkit

from InterNIC, the US Internet services organization, which covers browsers, searching tools, subject collections and 'what's new' sources.

Internet magazine's Website has a search tools page at

http://www.emap.com/Internet/search.html

that lists similar sources and e-mail address directories.

The *WebPlaces Internet Search Guide* at

http://www.webplaces.com/

covers a very wide range of services and is the place to find Cool Canadian Sites and Australia: Pick of the Day!

The US *PC Computing* magazine has its Map guide to the Internet at

http://www.zdnet.com/pccomp/lowband/webmap/spmaps/
map0896

It provides some very long lists that will keep you busy for days.

10

Keeping up with new resources

★ Printed sources
★ General services
★ Selective services
★ Specialist sources
★ Software agents

If you are a regular user of the Internet – perhaps monitoring how businesses are using the Net, checking details of new software or seeing which other organizations are researching in your subject area – then you may want to know about new resources quickly, rather than waiting until they reach subject collections or other directories.

However, keeping up with new resources on the Internet is not easy as hundreds of new Web sites, discussion lists, newsgroups and electronic journals can be added or amended each day. Here we discuss the most useful services that help you to keep uo-to-date – you will need to decide which ones will be of most value to you.

The popular UK Internet magazines like .net and Internet, and the computing sections of daily newspapers, make some attempt to list new services together with comments, but they can only be very selective in what they include and are not particularly oriented to academic material.

The most comprehensive and up-to-date listings of new resources are to be found on the Internet itself. You need to check

Web-based announcement services regularly for updates, but they have the advantage of offering direct links to the new services listed. Announcement services delivered by e-mail are more convenient, but can clog up your mailbox. You need to be very selective in using these services , as it is possible to spend a vast amount of time just looking at new Web pages, some of which may be of very marginal interest. Many quality Web sites (such as the subject gateways listed in Chapter 8) include a 'What's new' feature to let you know which new links have been added to them in the last week or so; your local university Web pages may do likewise. Possibly the most useful round-up of new resources for academic users is Heriot-Watt University's monthly *Internet Resources Newsletter* noted below.

Printed sources

The quality daily newspapers have weekly computing sections with news of new Web services: *The Guardian* (Thursday), *The Independent* (Monday), *The Times* (Wednesday) and the *Sunday Times*. Some of the contents are reproduced on the papers' Web sites (listed in Chapter 6). The major UK Internet magazines are listed in Chapter 13, and browsing through these can also be a useful way of keeping up-to-date with new sites. Again, they have Web sites which may include similar information. In addition, many general computer magazines such as *BYTE*, *Computer weekly* and *Personal computer world* regularly provide updates on new resources and Internet developments.

General sources with a broad coverage

Many services try to cover all subjects and types of source, but may be more or less comprehensive. Most are international in coverage, but some are limited or biased geographically.

The Heriot-Watt *Internet Resources Newsletter*
http://www.hw.ac.uk/libWWW/irn/irn.html
is a particularly useful source as it is produced monthly for the aca-

demic community in the UK by library staff at Heriot-Watt University. Subject-oriented resources are organized in sections by access method, with live links to the resources. However, there is a bias towards resources in science and technology, and business.

What's new in the UK

http://www.emap.com/whatsnew/xx1.htm

is a constantly updated list of new UK Websites from the publishers of *Internet* magazine.

What's new on the Internet: global edition

http://www.emap.com/whatsnew/global/

is similar to the above, but includes overseas sites.

What's new on Yahoo

http://www.yahoo.com/new/

is the most comprehensive guide: it consists of the new resources which have been added to the Yahoo subject collection. There are usually hundreds of items listed each day.

What's New Too!

http://newtoo.manifest.com/WhatsNewToo/index.html

is a similarly ambitious service claiming to post an average of over 500 new and unique announcements every day, within 36 hours of submission.

The *net-happenings* list is a busy, moderated, announcements-only distribution list which gathers announcements from many Internet sources and concentrates them into one list. There is a bias towards sites of educational value. *Net-happenings* is available as a discussion/distribution list (subscribe with the message: **subscribe net-happenings** to listserv@lists.internic.net), a newsgroup (**comp.internet.net-happenings**), and is archived on a Web server at

http://www.gi.net/NET/

The *comp.infosystems.www.announce* newsgroup, with around 50 postings per day, announces a wide range of new Web sites (academic, commercial, recreational). If you don't have local access to Usenet then try a public Usenet site (see Chapter 3).

Selective sources

The *NISS What's New* list
http://www.niss.ac.uk/welcome/whatsnew.html
is produced weekly. It lists significant new additions to the *NISS Information Gateway*, together with a brief description of the resource.

The *BUBL WWW/Gopher Subject Tree update*
http://www.bubl.bath.ac.uk/BUBL/subjnew.html
is produced weekly, listing additions and changes to the subject tree on the UK *BUBL Information Service*.

The *Scout Report*
http://rs.internic.net/scout/report
is a weekly publication offering a small selection of newly discovered Internet resources of interest to researchers and educators. A brief description of each new resource is given. It is accessed via the World Wide Web with links to all listed resources, or by subscribing to an e-mail distribution list (full details from Web page).

The *Netsurfer Digest* is an electronic magazine delivered by e-mail. Full subscription details are available from the Web page at
http://www.netsurf.com/nsd/index.html
A UK archive of past issues is at
http://cswww2.essex.ac.uk/Web/netsurfidx.html

Specialist sources

There are specialist sources for particular types of resource: discussion lists, electronic journals and telnet sites. As distribution-list-based services they deliver announcements of new services by e-mail. Further information and subscription details for these lists can be found from Diane Kovacs' *Directory of Scholarly and Professional E-Conferences* at
http://n2h2.com/KOVACS/

new-list Notification of new discussion lists world-wide.

new-lists Notification of new discussion lists for the UK higher education community.

newjour Notification of new electronic journals.

hytelnet Notification of new services added to Hytelnet (see Chapter 7).

Software agents

Intelligent agents are an increasingly used software solution to keeping up-to-date with new resources. You provide them with information about your interests, and then they use that information to make informed suggestions for other Internet resources that may also be of interest to you. Some of these products are available free of charge, but it is likely that commercial services that charge their users will become the norm.

So, for example, after creating a personal profile by selecting areas of interest listed in *What's New on the Web*

http://www.inet-access.net/~newonweb

you will be sent a daily customized e-mail message, tailored to your personal profile.

The online version of *The Times*

http://www.the-times.co.uk/

includes a feature called *The Personal Times*, which allows you to select those parts of the newspaper which most interest you, together with keywords, to put together a personalized newspaper.

Another approach is that of the *Firefly* personal software agent.

http://www.agents-inc.com/

It builds up a picture of your likes and dislikes (such as the type of music you like to listen to), and suggests other sources which you would enjoy and other people with similar tastes. You provide Firefly with your own ratings of information sources or categories on which it bases its recommendations.

11

How to create your own Web page

★ Why publish?
★ HTML outline
★ Guidelines on page design

Why publish?

These days any Internet user is able to be a publisher and have a potential readership of millions. Whether everyone *should* is, of course, another matter. Is there any benefit in putting up a personal home page with details of your interests and links to your favourite (or 'cool') Web sites if it includes little of real value? Creating Web pages about a particular band or sportsperson will have wider appeal, but isn't necessarily a good use of your institution's computer system! Universities and colleges will usually permit personal pages, but may limit the space that can be used and may close down services that create too much traffic on the local network. Thus Newcastle University had to close the Newcastle United Web site when the volume of use hindered academic use of the system, and the movie database at Cardiff had to move to a commercial Internet provider for the same reason.

However, there are useful 'approved' applications. You could:

★ make your CV available
★ detail the work of your research group
★ show images of work you have created, say in fine art or industrial design

★ make available software you have written
★ publish substantial information you have gathered on a topic
★ make available a database you have created.

You need to consider whether what you want to publish is original, interesting, accurate, up-to-date and in other ways worthwhile.

Remember that, as with e-mail, there are restrictions on what you may publish. Offensive, obscene, racist and libellous material is not allowed, and Web pages on academic systems should not be used for advertising or commercial purposes, nor should they include copyright material unless you have specific permission to do so. When requesting access to your local computer system you will have agreed to abide by local conditions of use, and once you are using JANET there is also the *JANET Acceptable Use Policy*

　　http://www.jnt.ac.uk/documents/use.html

These conditions are enforced. The general laws of a country apply too. Remember that you are publishing internationally, so what may be acceptable in one country may not be in another, for example blasphemy.

How to publish

Most people will make information available on the Internet by creating Web pages. How these are made available will vary between institutions depending on what sort of machine is used to host the pages (the Web server), so you will need to enquire, or you may find details on your local Web information service if you have one. On the other hand the procedures for creating pages are based on using the Hypertext Markup Language (HTML) and so are the same everywhere.

Hypertext Markup Language (HTML)

There is not space here to do more than give an outline of what HTML does, but it will be sufficient to allow you to create simple pages.

HTML is based on the principle of using tags, that is markers, to indicate the formatting and structure of text, placing of images and so on. This approach gives access to the information whatever the browser used, unlike a word-processed file or spreadsheet, which is accessible only to users with compatible software.

The layout that others will see is totally dependent on the tags and how the browser interprets them, not on how you lay out the page when you create it. Thus, text will flow continuously until told otherwise, and heading styles start where indicated and continue until the corresponding end-of-heading tag is reached. Different browsers will display the text in different ways, for example where line breaks occur or in the amount of space above or below headings. The file in HTML format will look very different from what is displayed, though it is helpful to you to put in plenty of spaces to see where the commands are. Your browser will normally allow you to see the HTML file for any page you are viewing – for example, in Netscape choose **View/Document Source**; in Lynx press the \ key. This is helpful in learning how HTML works.

HTML and browsers are developing all the time, and there will be new HTML features supported in only the latest versions of browsers. You may not be able to use the latest version and even if you can you should remember that many of your users will not be able to see your pages as you intended if you use features not generally supported, so don't be too adventurous.

Basic HTML tags

Tags are normally used in matched pairs, one to indicate the beginning of a particular feature and the other the end. So a main heading is defined by <H1> and </H1> – note the / in the end tag.

The major tags are

\<TITLE\>	\</TITLE\>	A title to the whole document
\<H1\> to \<H6\>	\</H1\> etc	Headings of various size – H1 is the largest
\<P\>	no end tag	New paragraph – add a line space and start a new line
\<BR\>	no end tag	Line break – start a new line
\<HR\>	no end tag	Draw a horizontal line (or rule)
\<UL\>	\</UL\>	An unordered (bulleted) list
\<OL\>	\</OL\>	An ordered (numbered) list
\<LI\>	no end tag	Item in a list
\<PRE\>	\</PRE\>	Preformatted text – preserves the layout, including spaces and tabs. Other tags cannot be used in such text. This provides a simple way of laying out tables, for example.

The title and other introductory material is usually enclosed by \<HEAD\> and \</HEAD\> and the rest of the page by \<BODY\> and \</BODY\>.

Tags can be in upper or lower case, but the convention is to use upper case.

If you want to link to other resources then you create a hyperlink in the form:

\<A HREF ="URL"\>*some text*\</A\> where *some text* is the highlighted link.

For example, if your document includes \<A HREF= "http://wxweb.msu.edu/weather"\>weather maps\</A\> then when the user clicks on the highlighted link text 'weather maps' the browser will display the page specified by the URL. If you are referring to a document on the same system as your pages you need give only the filename and not the complete URL.

Example

Figure 11.1 is a short piece of text in HTML, with Figure 11.2 showing how it might look with a graphical browser.

```
<BODY>

<H1>A brief guide to Internet  sources for chemistry and biomedical
sciences</H1>
<HR>

<H3>BIDS</H3>
<P>The BIDS service includes general databases and a number relating to
specific areas of chemistry - analytical, biotechnology, safety - and to
business aspects.
<UL>
<LI> <A HREF="http://www.bids.ac.uk">Background information</A>
 What's available. Documentation.
<LI> <A HREF="telnet://bids.ac.uk">Connect to BIDS</A> from here.
</UL>

<H3>Browsing subject collections</H3>

<UL>
<LI> <A HREF="http://www.shef.ac.uk/~chem/chemdex/">Chemdex</A>
at Sheffield University
<LI> <A HREF="http://www.indiana.edu:80/~cheminfo/">Cheminfo </A>at
Indiana University
<BODY>
```

Fig. 11.1 *Sample HTML file (body only)*

A brief guide to Internet sources for chemistry and biomedical sciences

BIDS

The BIDS service includes general databases and a number relating to specific areas of chemistry - analytical, biotechnology, safety - and to business aspects.

- Background information What's available. Documentation.
- Connect to BIDS from here.

Browsing subject collections

- Chemdex at Sheffield University
- Cheminfo at Indiana University

Fig. 11.2 *The HTML file as seen with a Web browser*

More commands

If you have a long document you can link to sections of it from a contents list at the top of the document. Insert at each section an 'anchor' in the form <A NAME=*"anchor"*>*some text*</A> You make a link to it from the heading in the contents list in the form <A HREF=*"#anchor"*>*some text*</A>

For example:

<LI><A HREF="#new">What's New on the Internet</A>
<H3><A NAME="new"></A>What's New on the Internet</H3>

links from 'What's new on the Internet' in the contents list to the section heading itself.

You may want to include images, such as photographs, icons, a logo, graphs, charts etc. These may be scanned images, created in a paint program, output from other software such as a spreadsheet, or copied from other Internet sources (but be aware of copyright). These images each have a filename and can be included in your pages by specifying them in the form:

<IMG SRC=*"image filename"* ALIGN=*position* ALT=*"some text"*>

ALIGN is optional and allows you to specify whether text in the same line should align with the *bottom*, *middle* or *top* of the image. ALT is also optional, but recommended, and gives some text, such as 'logo' or 'photograph', as an alternative for browsers that cannot show images.

If you want your image to be the hyperlink then the format is
<A HREF=*"URL"*><IMG SRC=*"image filename"* ALIGN=*position* ALT=*"some text"*></A>

Learning to use HTML

There are many more tags, for example for bold or italic text, background colours and patterns, tables, frames, adding video and sound, etc, and also facilities for designing interactive search forms. You can find out about these and more from the many books about the Web or HTML and from various comprehensive guides on the Web itself , such as

Beginner's guide to HTML
http://www.ncsa.uiuc.edu/General/Internet/WWW/HTML Primer.html

HTML quick reference
http://kuhttp.cc.ukans.edu/lynx_help/HTML_quick.html

How do they do that in HTML?
http://www.nashville.net/~carl/htmlguide

Though HTML documents can be created by text editors such as Windows Notepad or Emacs on Unix, you can see how tedious this would be for anything other than simple pages with few links. Fortunately there are editing tools you can use such as Internet Assistant (for Word for Windows v6.0) HoTMetaL, HTML Assistant, HotDog, WebAuthor and PageMill. These allow you to create the page the way you want it to look and the program then translates it into HTML for you. Tricky tags like hyperlinks can be created semi-automatically.

You will need to check with your computing service to see what is available to you.

Announcing your pages

Once created, your pages will be available to anyone using your university/college system and, provided access is not restricted to your campus only, eventually to users of search services. However, you may want to announce them to the world.

If they have a particular subject content you could send a message to an appropriate discussion list or newsgroup giving the URL and a brief description of the content. If there is a subject collection covering your topic you may wish to contact that too. You can also submit details to the general 'what's new' services discussed in the previous chapter.

For a list of places to announce pages see the FAQ: *How to announce your new Web site* distributed regularly on the **comp. infosystems.www.announce** newsgroup and also found at
   http://ep.com/faq/webannounce.html
and *Practical guide to announcing your World Wide Web* page at
   http://www.lawworld.com/pracprof/announce

Designing effective pages

You don't have to be a graphic designer to put together Web pages, but you do have to think about what will make them effective. Among useful guidelines are:

★ Make clear on the first page what the intention of your Web site is and what it contains.

★ If you want a maximum audience for your pages, then they should be predominantly plain text. If they are technically advanced and thus not viewable by everyone, tell users what browser is needed. Consider whether you need to offer a text version as an alternative.

★ Images make a page look more interesting but can take a long time to download, so don't include them unnecessarily. Consider using small ones – icons to decorate or 'thumbnail' pictures, especially to link to larger images. Don't have too many on any page.

★ Give alternative text to images, especially if the image is the hyperlink. Users of graphical browsers often have the images turned off for speed.

★ Backgrounds (plain or fancy) that obscure text, and text that blinks, may well annoy users.

★ Don't have a document of more than a few pages unless you have a contents list at the top with links to sections. Long documents are difficult to browse through.

★ Test your hyperlinks to ensure they work.

★ If you can, test your pages with different browsers and different versions, to see that they display as you intend. For example, Lynx displays italic text as underlined as if it were a link.

★ Make your pages consistent in style.

★ Include a date, your name and e-mail address.

★ Link to your institution's home pages.

You can, of course, find guidance online:

Guide to good practices for WWW authors
http://info.mcc.ac.uk/CGU/SIMA/Isaacs/toc.html

Yale C/AIM Web style manual
http://ukoln.bath.ac.uk/caim

The Web Developer's Virtual Library: style guidelines
http://WWW.Stars.com/Seminars/Style/

There are also Usenet groups and discussion lists that you can use to keep up with developments and to get help from other users. These include: **comp.infosystems.www.authoring.html**, **comp.infosystems.www.authoring.images** and the list **html-l** at **vm.ege.edu.tr**

Impressing your tutors – citing electronic sources in your work

When you complete an essay, dissertation or other piece of written work, you are usually expected to refer to (or cite) the publications you have used. This is to make it clear to anyone reading (and marking) the piece where your information has come from. These references need to be precise, giving the publication, date, pages, article title, etc, and there are standard ways of setting out references that you may be expected to use. So as you make more use of electronic sources, such as CD-ROM and the Internet, you need to refer to them in a similar way as to printed sources. Procedures for citing electronic sources are not yet as established as for printed sources, but there are some commonly used conventions.

As with citing printed sources, the important principle is to be consistent in the way you refer to the same sort of publication, and to include all the relevant detail needed to enable someone to find the source.

Generally recommended formats for citing Internet sources are:

E-mail correspondence

Author
Date (in round brackets)
Subject (underline or italics)
'e-mail to' recipient's name (in square brackets)
[online]

'Available e-mail:' recipient's e-mail address
Example: Corliss, B (16 September 1992) <u>News from Seattle</u>
[e-mail to T.Wright], [online]. Available e-mail:
twright@uvmvm.uvm.edu

Journal article from e-mail

Author
Title (not underlined or italicized)
Journal title (underlined or italics)
Type of medium (square brackets)
Volume (issue), date and paging (if given)
'Available e-mail:' e-mail address
Example: Sloan, B Crime statistics: how valid? <u>Social work review</u>
[online] 2(3) March 1995. Available e-mail: swr@howard.gov.uk

Discussion list message

Author
Date (round brackets)
Subject
Discussion-list name (underline or italics)
[online]
'Available e-mail:' e-mail address
Example: Roseman, M (7 June 1996) WWW guide for historians
<u>German-history discussion list</u> [online] Available e-mail: german-
history@mailbase.ac.uk

Complete discussion list

List name (underline or italic)
[online]
'Available e-mail:' e-mail address
Example: <u>Algeria news list</u> [online] Available e-mail: ALGE-
NEWS@gwuvm.gwu.edu

Usenet messages

Author
Date (round brackets)
Subject (underline or italics)
[discussion]
[online]
'Available Usenet newsgroup:' name of the group
Example: Tranholm, S (8 January 1993) <u>2001: a space odyssey</u> [discussion], [online] Available Usenet newsgroup: alt.cult-movies

FTP

Author
Date (that included with the source – round brackets)
Title (underline or italics)
[online]
'Available FTP:' address; directory; file
Example: King, ML (August 1963) <u>I have a dream</u> [online] Available FTP: mrcnext.cso.uiuc.edu Directory: gutenberg/freenet File: i-have-a-dream

Telnet

Author
Date (round brackets- put 'no date' if there is no date in the source)
Title (underline or italics)
[online]
'Available telnet:' address; directory: file
Example: Perot, R (1992) <u>An America in danger</u> [online] Available telnet: gopher.tc.umn.edu Directory: libraries/electronic books File: An America in Danger

World Wide Web

Title (underline or italics)
URL
Example: PC magazine URL: http://www.ziff.com/~pcmag
If you need further guidance ask your library staff or see if the library has the following book:

Li, X & Crane, N *Electronic Styles: An Expanded Guide to Citing Electronic Information* 2nd edn, Information Today, 1996.
   Excerpts from the book can be found at
   http://www.uvm.edu/~xli/reference/estyles.html
There is an online *Guide to Citing Internet Sources* at
   http://www.bournemouth.ac.uk/service-
   depts/lis/LIS_Pub/harvardsystint.html

13

What next?

★ Local support
★ Online guides
★ Books and magazines

Local support

This book can only discuss the Internet in general terms. Staff at your institution can provide specific information on which services are available to you and how to use them. Either the library or the computing centre is likely to provide local documentation (increasingly published on the local Web pages), and may run demonstrations or courses about the Internet. In particular, they may offer training material produced as part of the *Netskills* initiative (see below). Commercial Internet training is expensive, so do take advantage of the assistance and resources freely provided while you are a student!

If you are not sure where to start, ask at the Help or Enquiry points in the library or computer centre.

Online guides

TONIC

The Online Netskills Interactive Course (TONIC)
   http://www.netskills.ac.uk/TONIC/
is a Web-based learning course on using the Internet produced by Netskills, a project that is creating Internet training material for

UK higher education. TONIC is an easy-to-understand, structured course, offering step-by-step practical guidance on major Internet topics, progressing from basic through to advanced. The course as a whole is intended for beginners to networking who have some familiarity with computers. The course provides an introduction to the Internet and computer networks in general, describing and illustrating the main software tools for navigating the networks. However, these tools are only a means to an end, the end being the wealth of information and communication resources offered via the networks. The course looks at types and examples of networked information, at the means for searching that information, and at the communication facilities and resources on the Net.

The course is designed to give the user practice with using various Internet services, and to provide feedback on progress. There are exercises, simulations, animations, optional self-assessment tests, and the opportunity to e-mail your comments. A system of registration makes it possible for you to follow through the course in a systematic way, and to go straight to the point where you left off in a previous session. Helpful links to orient you and to enable you to take alternative paths through the material are provided throughout.

Internet Roadmap (Patrick Crispen)

This six-week course is 'designed to teach new "Net travellers" how to travel around the rapidly expanding (and often confusing) "Information Superhighway" without getting lost'. It comprises 27 individual lessons, and provides a comprehensive guide to the Internet and the tools used to access the information available on it. Although you are encouraged to follow the course from beginning to end, it is possible to dip into specific sections that interest you. Each lesson comes with 'homework', designed to encourage you to explore the Internet for yourself.

You can receive the lessons by e-mail by sending the message **subscribe roadmap96 to listserv@lists.internic.net**

or see them on the web at
http://rs.internic.net/roadmap96

John December's Internet Web Text

Internet Web Text
http://www.december.com/web/text/index.html
is a meta-resource or 'one-stop' site for both new and experienced
Internet users. This hypertext guide was created as a required 'text'
for a course on computer-mediated communication that the author
was teaching, and it provides a 'launching pad for learning about,
exploring, and searching the Internet'.

Internet Web Text is divided into seven sections covering: orien-
tation, Internet guides, reference materials, browsing and exploring
tools, subject- and word-oriented searching, and information about
connecting with people. Rather than simply giving lists of
resources, December comments on the resources and documents
listed, and offers advice on which resources might be most appropriate in different situations.

The pages provide an excellent introduction to the Internet, and
can be used as a self-paced guide – perhaps exploring one section a
week. The site is updated regularly. Internet Web Text also offers
links to other Web sites December has developed on computer-mediated communication (CMC), CMC studies, and Internet tools.

EFF's (Extended) Guide to the Internet

Although becoming dated, EFF's *(Extended) Guide to the Internet*
(formerly known as 'Big Dummy's Guide to the Internet') was
written by Adam Gaffin for a joint project of Apple Computer Inc.
and The Electronic Frontier Foundation (EFF). The online version
is available at:
http://www.eff.org/papers/eegtti/eegttitop.html

Books

Publishing books about the Internet is certainly a growth industry. Your library is likely to hold a number of relevant titles, and doing a keyword or subject search on 'Internet' or 'Web' in the library catalogue should retrieve most of them. If you decide to buy a book about the Internet (in addition to this one!), do be cautious, as price is no indication of quality. Always ensure that you have purchased the most up-to-date edition — you can check details at the *Computer Manuals Online Bookstore*

> **http://www.compman.co.uk**

or *The Internet Bookshop*

> **http://www/bookshop.co.uk**

Do look at the contents of the book before purchase – if you are concerned with accessing the Internet through JANET, you will not need to pay for pages discussing which Information Service Provider (ISP) to select, nor will you require an extensive knowledge of Unix unless you plan to run your own server. A book which merely lists the URLs of Internet resources will quickly date – it is much better to consult the library copy of a *Yellow pages* guide to Internet resources. One useful reference book which your library may hold is the *Gale guide to Internet databases* edited by Joanna Zakalik.

Very few books are written in the UK, but there is a trend to 'repackage' books published in North America for the UK market, although in some cases only the price and cover are changed! While the authors listed below are North American, they are nevertheless recommended for the content and clarity of their works.

Recommended authors: John December, Paul Gilster, Harley Hahn, Ed Krol, Tracy LaQuey, and Roy Tennant.

Popular magazines

There are a growing number of UK Internet magazines. They will contain Internet news, product reviews, lists of new resources, answers to readers' queries, guides to sources on specific topics and so on, although the emphasis is mostly on the recreational uses of the Net. Do check to see if your library (or a local public library) subscribes, as they cost around £3–£4 an issue, and much of the information dates quickly. Their Web sites, listed below, will indicate the coverage and content of the magazines, and these sites are a useful source for news items in themselves, usually including some of the contents of each issue.

.net (Future Publishing)
http://www.futurenet.co.uk/

Internet: the essential guide (EMAP)
http://www.emap.com/internet/

Internet Today (Paragon Publishing)
http://www.paragon.co.uk/it/index.html

Internet World (Meckler)
http://www.internetworld.com/

Netuser (Paragon Publishing)
http://www.paragon.co.uk/netuser/index.html

Wired (published in both a UK and US version by Wired Ventures Ltd)
http://www.hotwired.com/frontdoor/

These magazines are also particularly useful for providing up-to-date information on pricing and options offered by commercial Internet Service Providers (ISPs), if you wish to continue access the Internet once you leave higher education.

Now it's up to you . . .

The book will have given you an outline of what the Internet is, and an indication of what it can be used for. We have included details of many information sources, and information on how to locate others. In this final chapter we have given further suggestions on how you may develop to a greater depth the skills and knowledge discussed throughout the book. If you have used the Internet before, then we hope you can use this book to learn of new sources and services. If you are a newcomer to the Net, then now is the time to take the plunge – if that is the right word – and start exploring. This book is a guide to help you to see what the Internet can do for you – your only limitations are your imagination and the time available to you!

14

Jargon explained

Archie. Utility that maintains a searchable database of the contents of **file archive** sites.

AHDS (Arts and Humanities Data Service). Information services for UK higher education.

ASCII (American Standard Code for Information Interchange). Standard way of encoding characters, numbers and symbols. Plain text files are sometimes referred to as ASCII.

BIDS (Bath Information and Data Services). A range of services, especially bibliographic databases, for UK higher education.

binary. Notation using only the digits 0 and 1 – the simplest form used by a computer. Files retrieved by **FTP** may often be in binary.

browser. Software to view **World Wide Web** documents. Examples include Netscape Navigator and Microsoft Internet Explorer for graphical use, and Lynx for text only.

compression. Procedures to pack files into a smaller size to reduce storage requirements and speed up transfer across networks. Filenames for compressed files have extensions such as .zip and .tor. Compressed files must be uncompressed before they can be used.

conferencing. Using **discussion lists** and **newsgroups** to communicate, share information or debate particular subjects.

CWIS (Campus Wide Information Service). Information service for members of a university or college. Now usually offered using the **World Wide Web**.

dataset. Collection of numerical and bibliographic data made available for searching across the Internet. UK examples are *BIDS* and *MIDAS*.

discussion list. E-mail-based subject **conference.**

domain name. Unique alphabetic representation of a computer's location on the Internet. Compare **IP address.** The Domain Name System (DNS) is the database of all domain names.

EDINA. Information services for UK higher education provided from Edinburgh University.

e-mail (electronic mail). System which enables messages to be sent from one person's computer (or space on a central computer) to another.

FAQ (Frequently Asked Questions). Common questions and answers about a particular topic are often collected in a FAQ file, which is updated as necessary and reissued periodically, commonly on a **newsgroup.**

file archive. Collection of files - such as software, numerical data, texts - that can be retrieved by **FTP.**

FTP (File Transfer Protocol). A standard **protocol** (and an application) which permits files to be copied from one computer to another, regardless of file format or operating system.

gopher. Utility that organizes information in hierarchical ways and also allows users to retrieve and view text information from **servers** on the Internet.

GUI (Graphical User Interface). A graphical way of using computers that involves using a mouse to make choices, rather than keying commands. Microsoft Windows and Netscape Navigator are examples.

host: A computer system which provides a service, such as **electronic mail** or access to a database.

HTML (Hypertext Markup Language). The coding system used for creating documents on the **World Wide Web** that can be read using a **browser.**

HTTP (Hypertext Transfer Protocol). The search and retrieval **protocol** used for transferring **HTML** documents.

hypertext. Text that contains links to other text, allowing information to be retrieved nonsequentially.

hypermedia. Electronic media – text, graphics, video, sound –

linked to provide information.

Internet. The world-wide collection of interconnected computer networks.

IP address. Unique numeric representation of a computer's location on the Internet. It comprises four sets of numbers separated by periods. Compare **domain name.**

JANET (Joint Academic Network). The computer network linking UK higher and further education institutions and research organizations.

Java. A programming language that can be used to create applications such as animation and multimedia for Web pages.

Listserv. A common **utility** used to manage **discussion lists** on the Internet.

Lynx. A text-only Web **browser**.

Mailbase. The organization which manages and promotes the use of **discussion lists** for UK higher education.

MIDAS (Manchester Information Datasets and Associated Services). A service for UK higher education providing economic and social statistics.

Netscape. The company producing Netscape Navigator, the most common graphical **browser** for the World Wide Web. The browser itself is usually referred to just as Netscape.

newsgroups. The hierarchically arranged collection of topic areas in **Usenet**.

newsreader. Software needed to read **newsgroups**.

NISS (National Information Services and Systems). The organization providing the *NISS Information Gateway* service for UK education.

OPAC (Online Public Access Catalogue). A contrived name for a computerized library catalogue.

port. A connection to a computer system, through which data can be exchanged.

protocol. A well-defined set of data-exchange rules that apply to communication between computer systems.

search engine. Software that searches a database. Commonly to describe services that search the content of the **World Wide Web**.

server. A computer which provides software and services across a local, national or international network.

SuperJANET. The upgraded version of **JANET** that has greater speed and capacity, particularly for transmitting still and moving images and sound.

telnet. A standard **protocol** (and an application) that permits a user to log onto a remote computer system.

tool. Another word for **utility**.

Unix. A computer operating system that is commonly used on machines offering Internet services.

URL (Uniform Resource Locator). Standard naming/addressing system for files on the **Internet**.

Usenet. Worldwide **conferencing** system comprising thousands of **newsgroups** on a huge range of subjects.

utility. A program for a particular small task, such as managing **e-mail** or creating **HTML** text.

Veronica (Very Easy Rodent-Oriented Net-wide Index of Computerized Archives) (!) A means of searching **gopher** menu titles world-wide.

VRML (Virtual Reality Modelling Language). The programming language used to create virtual reality applications across the Internet.

VT100. A standard for terminal display that is usually needed for **telnet** connections.

WAIS (Wide-Area Information Server). A means of indexing and searching text files on the Internet. Less commonly used than it was.

WWW (World Wide Web). The part of the Internet consisting of **hypermedia**, and needing a **browser** to view its pages.

For an extensive glossary of terms see *ILC Glossary of Internet Terms*
http://www.matisse.net/files/glossary.html

Index